Differential Privacy

From Theory to Practice

Synthesis Lectures on Information Security, Privacy, & Trust

Editor
Elisa Bertino, *Purdue University*
Ravi Sandhu, *University of Texas, San Antonio*

The Synthesis Lectures Series on Information Security, Privacy, and Trust publishes 50- to 100-page publications on topics pertaining to all aspects of the theory and practice of Information Security, Privacy, and Trust. The scope largely follows the purview of premier computer security research journals such as ACM Transactions on Information and System Security, IEEE Transactions on Dependable and Secure Computing and Journal of Cryptology, and premier research conferences, such as ACM CCS, ACM SACMAT, ACM AsiaCCS, ACM CODASPY, IEEE Security and Privacy, IEEE Computer Security Foundations, ACSAC, ESORICS, Crypto, EuroCrypt and AsiaCrypt. In addition to the research topics typically covered in such journals and conferences, the series also solicits lectures on legal, policy, social, business, and economic issues addressed to a technical audience of scientists and engineers. Lectures on significant industry developments by leading practitioners are also solicited.

Analysis Techniques for Information Security
Anupam Datta, Somesh Jha, Ninghui Li, David Melski, and Thomas Reps
2010

Operating System Security
Trent Jaeger
2008

Differential Privacy: From Theory to Practice

Ninghui Li, Min Lyu, Dong Su, and Weining Yang

ISBN: 978-3-031-01222-8   paperback
ISBN: 978-3-031-02350-7   ebook
ISBN: 978-3-031-00235-9   hardcover

DOI 10.1007/978-3-031-02350-7

A Publication in the Springer series
SYNTHESIS LECTURES ON INFORMATION SECURITY, PRIVACY, & TRUST

Lecture #18
Series Editors: Elisa Bertino, *Purdue University*
                Ravi Sandhu, *University of Texas, San Antonio*
Series ISSN
Print 1945-9742   Electronic 1945-9750

Differential Privacy

From Theory to Practice

Ninghui Li
Purdue University

Min Lyu
University of Science and Technology of China

Dong Su
Purdue University

Weining Yang
Purdue University

SYNTHESIS LECTURES ON INFORMATION SECURITY, PRIVACY, &
TRUST #18

ABSTRACT

Over the last decade, differential privacy (DP) has emerged as the *de facto* standard privacy notion for research in privacy-preserving data analysis and publishing. The DP notion offers strong privacy guarantee and has been applied to many data analysis tasks.

This Synthesis Lecture is the first of two volumes on differential privacy. This lecture differs from the existing books and surveys on differential privacy in that we take an approach balancing theory and practice. We focus on empirical accuracy performances of algorithms rather than asymptotic accuracy guarantees. At the same time, we try to explain why these algorithms have those empirical accuracy performances. We also take a balanced approach regarding the semantic meanings of differential privacy, explaining both its strong guarantees and its limitations.

We start by inspecting the definition and basic properties of DP, and the main primitives for achieving DP. Then, we give a detailed discussion on the the semantic privacy guarantee provided by DP and the caveats when applying DP. Next, we review the state of the art mechanisms for publishing histograms for low-dimensional datasets, mechanisms for conducting machine learning tasks such as classification, regression, and clustering, and mechanisms for publishing information to answer marginal queries for high-dimensional datasets. Finally, we explain the sparse vector technique, including the many errors that have been made in the literature using it.

The planned Volume 2 will cover usage of DP in other settings, including high-dimensional datasets, graph datasets, local setting, location privacy, and so on. We will also discuss various relaxations of DP.

KEYWORDS

privacy, anonymization

Contents

Acknowledgments

We thank Professor Elisa Bertino for encouraging us to write this Synthesis Lecture. This lecture is based upon work partially supported by the National Science Foundation under Grant No. 1116991. Any opinions, findings, and conclusions or recommendations expressed in this lecture are those of the author(s) and do not necessarily reflect the views of the National Science Foundation.

Ninghui Li, Min Lyu, Dong Su, and Weining Yang
October 2016

CHAPTER 1

Introduction

Data collected by organizations and agencies are a key resource in today's information age. However, the disclosure of those data poses serious threats to individual privacy. A fundamental challenge is to balance privacy and utility in data sharing. There are two main research problems. First, what should be the definition of privacy? Second, given a privacy definition, for a given task, what algorithms can provide the highest utility while providing a certain level of privacy protection? These topics have been studied for decades, involving multiple research communities.

In recent years, Differential Privacy (DP) is increasingly being accepted as the privacy notion of choice. Informally, the DP notion requires any single element in a dataset to have only a limited impact on the output. A large body of literature on DP is being built up. A book titled *Algorithmic Foundations of Differential Privacy* [Dwork and Roth, 2013], published in 2014, gives a survey of the field from a theoretical point of view.

We were motivated to write this book for several reasons. First and foremost, we want to provide a comprehensive survey on research in DP from a more practical perspective. Dwork and Roth [2013] and most of the current surveys on DP [Dwork, 2008, Dwork and Smith, 2010, Ji et al., 2014] are written from theoreticians' point of view. They presented mostly results obtained from a pure theoretical approach. In a pure theoretical approach, one aims at proving asymptotic utility guarantees for proposed methods. This often results in methods that have limited applicability to practical scenarios for a number of reasons. First, a method with an appealing asymptotic utility guarantee can (and often does) underperform naive methods except for very large parameters, where the method requires time and space resources that are too large to be feasible. Second, asymptotic analysis ignores constants (and oftentimes poly-logarithmic terms as well), whereas very significant improvements can result from reducing the constants, and these constants often constitute the main differences between the competing best-performing methods. Third, as the utility guarantee must hold for all datasets (including pathological ones), such guarantees are typically so loose that they are meaningless once the actual parameters are plugged in.

Indeed, the best performing algorithms for most of the data analysis tasks are often not included in these existing surveys. We want to point out that a purely experimental approach of presenting experimental results as validation without any analysis is also problematic. As there are many tunable parameters, it is often possible to reach conflicting conclusions just by choosing parameters differently. Without some theoretical understanding of these parameters, experimental results alone say very little.

In this book we try to walk a middle road between theory and practice, and focus on techniques and mechanisms that have been applied in *experimental settings*, by which we mean that they have been implemented and experimentally evaluated. This motivation can be captured by the famous quote: **In theory, there is no difference between theory and practice. But, in practice, there is.**

The second main motivation behind this book is to provide a balanced examination of the power and limitation of DP. There is an ongoing debate about the meaning and value of DP. Some argue that the notion of DP offers strong privacy protection regardless of the adversary's prior knowledge, while enabling all kinds of data analysis. Others offer criticisms regarding DP's privacy guarantee and utility limitations. We believe that the truth is more nuanced than either extreme. While DP has a lot of potential, it is often applied incorrectly, and in several settings (especially for high-dimensional datasets), we still lack effective techniques to protect data privacy while preserving utility.

1.1   PRIVACY VIOLATION INCIDENTS

Defining data privacy is difficult. One reason is that it is desired that some information about the data is revealed; otherwise, one simply deletes the data (or does not collect it in the first place). It is often debatable whether revealing certain information compromises privacy or not. We now examine several well-known privacy incidents. This provides concrete contexts when we talk about privacy definitions. Furthermore, similar to other contexts in security and privacy, the concept of privacy is easier to define by identifying what are privacy breaches. Privacy can then be simply defined by requiring that no privacy breach occurs. As privacy is a social concept, any formalization of privacy violation must be based on what the society perceives as privacy breaches. From these well-publicized privacy incidents in data publishing, we identify the common features of what the society considers to be privacy breaches. We show that the disclosures in these incidents all fall into a general class that we call positive membership disclosures. In such a disclosure, when given the published dataset, an adversary can find an entity and assert with high confidence that the entity's data is in the original dataset.

1.1.1   PRIVACY INCIDENTS

An early and well-publicized privacy incident is from the supposedly anonymized medical visit data made available by the Group Insurance Commission (GIC) (Sweeney [2002]). While the obvious personal identifiers are removed, the published data included zip code, date of birth, and gender, which are sufficient to uniquely identify a significant fraction of the population. Sweeney [2002] showed that by correlating this dataset with the publicly available Voter Registration List for Cambridge, Massachusetts, medical visits about many individuals can be easily identified, including those of William Weld, a former governor of Massachusetts. We note that even without access to the public voter registration list, the same privacy breaches can occur. Many individuals' birthdate, gender, and zip code are public information. This is especially the case with the advent of social networking sites, including Facebook, where users share seemingly innocuous personal information to the public.

Another well-known privacy incident came from publishing web search logs. In 2006, AOL released three months of search logs involving 650,000 users. The main privacy protection technique used is replacing user ids with random numbers. This proved to be a failure. Two *New York Times* journalists, Barbaro and Tom Zeller [2006], were able to re-identify Thelma Arnold, a 62-year-old women living in Lilburn, GA, from the published search logs. Ms. Arnold's search log includes her last name and location names near where she lived. The reporters were able to cross-reference this information with phonebook entries. After the *New York Times* article had been published, the data was immediately retracted by AOL. Later a class action lawsuit was filed against AOL. This scandal led to the resignation of AOL's CTO and the dismissal of two employees.

In 2009, Netflix released a dataset containing the movie rating data from 500,000 users as part of a one-million dollar challenge to the data mining research community for developing effective algorithms for predicting users' movie preferences based on their viewing history and ratings. While the data was anonymized in order to protect users' privacy, Narayanan and Shmatikov [2008] showed that an adversary having some knowledge about a subscriber's movie viewing experience can easily identify the subscriber's record if present in the dataset. For example, Narayanan and Shmatikov [2008] showed that, from the profiles of 50 IMDB users, at least two of them also appear in the Netflix dataset.

Another privacy incident targeted the Genome-Wide Association Studies (GWAS). These studies normally compare the DNA sequences of two groups of participants: people with the disease (cases) and similar people without (controls). Each person's DNA mutations (single-nucleotide polymorphisms, or SNPs) at indicative locations are read, and this information is then analyzed. Traditionally, researchers publish aggregate frequencies of SNPs for participants in the two groups. In 2008, Homer et al. [2008] proposed attacks that could tell with high confidence whether an individual is in the case group, assuming that the individual's DNA is known. The attack works even if the group includes hundreds of individuals. Because of the privacy concerns from such attacks, a number of institutions, including the U.S. National Institute of Health (NIH) and the Wellcome Trust in London all decided to restrict access to data from GWAS. Such attacks need access to the victim's DNA data and publicly available genomic database to establish the likely SNP frequencies in the general population.

Another example of the failure of naive "data anonymization" is location-based social networks that provide friend discovery feature by location proximity, documented by Li et al. [2014b]. These social networks try to provide some privacy protection by using a number of location-obfuscating techniques. One technique is to show to a user only relative distances of other users to her, instead of their location coordinates. Another is to set a limit on the precision of the reported information. For example, Skout defines localization accuracy to 1 mile, i.e., users will be located with an accuracy no better than 1 mile. Similarly, Wechat and Momo set 100 m and 10 m as their localization accuracy limits. Yet another technique is to restrict a user's view to within a certain distance of the user, or to no more than a certain number of users. Li et al. [2014b] demonstrated the effectiveness of attacks that use lots of fake locations to issue many queries and then aggregate this information to infer the exact locations of users.

1.1.2   LESSONS FROM PRIVACY INCIDENTS

From these incidents we learn the following lessons.

Re-identification matters. In the GIC, AOL, and Netflix incidents, one is able to correctly identify *one individual*'s record from supposedly anonymous data. This fact alone is sufficient for the society to agree that privacy is breached. It does not matter whether an adversary has learned additional sensitive information about the individual.

Positive assertion of membership matters. In the GWAS example, only aggregate information is published and there is no individual record for re-identification to occur. However, so long as the adversary can positively assert that one individual's data is in the input dataset based on the output, this is considered a privacy breach.

Must protect everyone. In several attacks, only a single individual is re-identified; however, that is sufficient to cause widespread privacy concerns and serious consequences (e.g., the AOL case). This suggests that privacy protection must apply to *every individual*. A method that on average offers good protection, but may compromise some individual's privacy, is not acceptable.

No separation of quasi-identifier and sensitive attributes. A lot of database privacy research assumes the division of all attributes into quasi-identifiers (QIDs) and sensitive attributes (SA), where the adversary is assumed to know the QIDs, but not SAs. This separation, however, is very hard to obtain in practice. No such separation exists in the cases of AOL, Netflix, or GWAS. Even though only some attributes are used in the GIC incident, it is difficult to assume that they are the only QIDs. Other attributes in the GIC data includes visit date, diagnosis, etc. There may well exist an adversary who knows this information about some individuals, and if with this knowledge these individuals' record can be re-identified, it is still a serious privacy breach. The same difficulty is true for publishing any kind of census, medical, or transactional data. When publishing anonymized microdata, one has to defend against all kinds of adversaries, some know one set of attributes, and others know a different set. An attribute about one individual may be known to some adversaries, and unknown (and thus should be considered sensitive) to other adversaries. In summary, one should assume that for every individual, there may exist an adversary who knows *all attributes* of that individual, but is unsure about the membership, i.e., whether that individual's data is included in the dataset or not. Defining privacy as protecting memebership under such a strong adversary model is more appropriate than identifying what sensitive information about an individual needs to be protected.

1.2   ON BALANCING THEORY AND PRACTICE

A paradoxical phenomenon in research on differentially private data analysis and publishing is that most algorithms that have a theorem proving its utility perform poorly in practice, which means that the error bounds in the theorems are too big to be relevant. On the other hand, most algorithms that perform well in experimental evaluations tend not to have any meaningful utility theorem. An illustrating example of this is the Multiplicative Weights Exponential Mechanism (MWEM) in Hardt et al. [2012]. This mechanism aims at publishing an approximation of the input dataset D so that counting queries in a given set Q can be answered accurately. One answers queries in Q by starting from an uninformative approximation of D and iteratively improving this approximation. In each iteration, one computes answers for all queries in Q using the current approximation, then uses the exponential mechanism to privately select one query q from Q that has the most error, then obtains a new answer to $q(D)$ in a way that satisfies the privacy, and finally updates the approximation with this new query/answer pair. This update uses the multiplicative weight update method (Arora et al. [2012]). For example, assuming that the approximation is in the form of a histogram, and the estimated answer for q based on the current approximation is less than the new answer, then the update scales up all bins that are included in q by multiplying a factor, and normalizes the histogram.

Given T rounds, a basic version of MWEM keeps all $T+1$ versions of the approximation, and performs a single update with each new query/answer pair. Finally, for each query it uses the average of the answers obtained from all $T+1$ approximations. This does not fully utilize the information obtained from the query/answer pairs. The more practical method proposed in Hardt et al. [2012] uses two improvements. First, in each round, after obtaining a new query/answer pair, it goes through **all** known query/answer pairs over 100 iterations to do multiplicative updates; this causes the approximation to come close to a state that is consistent with all known query/answer pairs. Second, it uses the last, and almost certainly the most accurate approximation to answer all queries. While the two improvements provide much better empirical accuracy, they are done "at the expense of the theoretical guarantees" [Hardt et al., 2012], because a utility theorem is proven for the basic version, but no utility theorem is proven for the improved version, the version that actually works!

A large part of the reason is that theoretical analysis can only be applied to algorithms that are simple, e.g., doing only one round of multiplicative update instead of 100 rounds. On the other hand, well-performing algorithms are likely difficult to analyze in the traditional framework, because they tend to exploit features that are satisfied by common datasets, but can be violated by pathological examples.

For another example, consider Frequent Itemset Mining (FIM). In Bhaskar et al. [2010], a formal definition of utility, (δ, η)-useful for FIM, was introduced. In Zeng et al. [2012], it is proven that for an ϵ-DP algorithm which is (δ, η)-useful for reasonable choice of δ, η, the ϵ must be over a certain value. Given the parameters from commonly used datasets, the bounds on ϵ have to be so large that they provide no meaningful privacy. This, however, does not prevent several algorithms for FIM from performing quite well empirically on datasets commonly used as benchmarks for FIM, e.g., Li et al. [2012b], Zeng et al. [2012]. These methods, however, lack meaningful formal utility theorems.

In this book, we advocate the method of conducting semi-formal analysis of a method's utility, combined with experimental validation of the analysis. Such analysis often consists of analyzing the scale of noises in different steps, how they are affected by different parameters, and how they impact the performance. The analysis is less formal than a utility theorem, and requires experimental results to support. However, such analysis is a better indicator of whether a method works in practice or not.

1.3 ORGANIZATION OF THIS BOOK

Because of space limit, this is only Volume 1 of the book. Volume 1 has the following chapters:

- Chapter 2 gives definition, basic properties, and the main primitives for satisfying ϵ-DP.

- Chapter 3 discusses exactly what ϵ-DP mean, including semantic privacy guarantees provided by ϵ-DP and the caveats when applying ϵ-DP.

- Chapter 4 presents mechanisms for publishing histograms for low-dimensional datasets.

- Chapter 5 presents mechanisms for conducting machine learning algorithms while satisfying ϵ-DP. Such problems can be formulated as optimization problems.

- Chapter 6 presents algorithms for publishing information to answer marginal queries for higher-dimensional datasets.

- Chapter 7 presents the Sparse Vector Technique, which is a basic technique for satisfying differential privacy on answering queries.

1.4 TOPICS FOR VOLUME 2

Topics that we plan to cover the Volume 2 include the following:

- Methods for the local privacy setting, which does not assume a trusted third party.

- High-dimensional transactional datasets, especially finding frequent itemsets.

- Graph datasets.

- The notion of (ϵ, δ)-DP, which relaxes ϵ-DP.

- Other relaxation of DP, such as the membership privacy framework.

- Application of DP and DP-like privacy notions in location privacy.

CHAPTER 2

A Primer on ϵ-Differential Privacy

2.1 THE DEFINITION OF ϵ-DP

Informally, the DP notion requires any single element in a dataset to have only a limited impact on the output. The following definition is taken from Dwork [2006] and Dwork et al. [2006].

Definition 2.1 ϵ-Differential Privacy. An algorithm $\mathcal{A}$ satisfies ϵ-differential privacy (ϵ-DP), where $\epsilon \geq 0$, if and only if for any datasets D and D' that *differ on one element*, we have

$$\forall T \subseteq Range(\mathcal{A}) : \ \Pr\left[\mathcal{A}(D) \in T\right] \leq e^{\epsilon} \Pr\left[\mathcal{A}(D') \in T\right], \tag{2.1}$$

where $Range(\mathcal{A})$ denotes the set of all possible outputs of the algorithm $\mathcal{A}$.

The condition (2.1) can be equivalently stated as:

$$\forall t \in Range(\mathcal{A}) : \ \frac{\Pr\left[\mathcal{A}(D) = t\right]}{\Pr\left[\mathcal{A}(D') = t\right]} \leq e^{\epsilon}, \tag{2.2}$$

where we define $\frac{0}{0}$ to be 1.

More generally, ϵ-DP can be defined by requiring Eq. (2.1) to hold on D and D' that are *neighboring*. When applying DP, an important choice is the precise condition under which D and D' are considered to be neighboring. Even when applying DP to relational datasets and interpreting "differing by one element" as "differing by a single record (or tuple)," there are still two natural choices, which lead to what are called unbounded and bounded DP in Kifer and Machanavajjhala [2011]. In *Unbounded DP*, D and D' are neighboring if D can be obtained from D' by adding or removing one element. In *Bounded DP*, D and D' are neighboring if D can be obtained from D' by replacing one element in D' with another element. When using bounded DP, two datasets that have different number of elements are not considered to be neighboring; therefore, publishing the exact number of elements in the input dataset satisfies ϵ-DP for any ϵ under bounded DP. However, doing so does not satisfy ϵ-DP for any ϵ in unbounded DP.

One way to understand the intuition of DP is the following "opting-out" analogy. We want to publish $\mathcal{A}(D)$, where D consists of data of many individuals. An individual objects to publishing $\mathcal{A}(D)$ because her data is in D and she is concerned about her privacy. In this case, we can address the individual's privacy concern by removing her data from D (or replacing her data with some arbitrary value) to obtain D' and publishing $\mathcal{A}(D')$. However, achieving privacy protection by removing an individual's data is infeasible. Since we need to protect everyone's privacy, following this approach means that we would need to remove everyone's data. DP tries to approximate the effect of opting out, by ensuring that any effect due to the inclusion of one's data is small. This is achieved by ensuring that for any output, one will see the same output with a similar probability even if any single individual's data is removed (unbounded DP), or replaced (bounded DP).

2.1.1   BOUNDED DP OR UNBOUNDED DP

In the literature, it is generally assumed that using either bounded or unbounded DP is fine, and one can choose whichever one that is more convenient. We point out, however, that using bounded DP is problematic. More specifically, as we show in Section 2.2, bounded DP does not compose under parallel composition (whereas unbounded DP does). This parallel composition property is often used when proving that an algorithm satisfies ϵ-DP.

We also note that any algorithm that satisfies ϵ-unbounded DP also satisfies (2ϵ)-bounded DP, since replacing one element with another can be achieved by removing one element and then adding the other. Therefore, we use unbounded DP in this book.

2.2   PROPERTIES OF ϵ-DP

DP is an appealing privacy notion in part because it has the following properties. These properties are very useful when designing multi-step algorithms that satisfy ϵ-DP.

2.2.1   POST-PROCESSING AND SEQUENTIAL COMPOSITION

One important property of ϵ-DP is that given an algorithm that satisfies ϵ-DP, no matter what additional processing one performs on the output of the algorithm, the composition of the algorithm and the post-processing step still satisfies ϵ-DP.

Proposition 2.2 Post-processing *Given $\mathcal{A}_1(\cdot)$ that satisfies ϵ-DP, then for any (possibly randomized) algorithm $\mathcal{A}_2$, the composition of $\mathcal{A}_1$ and $\mathcal{A}_2$, i.e., $\mathcal{A}_2(\mathcal{A}_1(\cdot))$ satisfies ϵ-DP.*

Proof. Let D and D' be any two neighboring databases. Let $\mathcal{S}$ be $Range(\mathcal{A}_1)$. For any $t \in Range(\mathcal{A}_2)$, we have

$$\Pr[\mathcal{A}_2(\mathcal{A}_1(D)) = t] = \sum_{s \in \mathcal{S}} \Pr[\mathcal{A}_1(D) = s] \Pr[\mathcal{A}_2(s) = t]$$
$$\leq \sum_{s \in \mathcal{S}} e^\epsilon \Pr[\mathcal{A}_1(D') = s] \Pr[\mathcal{A}_2(s) = t]$$
$$= e^\epsilon \Pr[\mathcal{A}_2(\mathcal{A}_1(D')) = t].$$

If $\mathcal{S}$ is not countable, $\Pr[\mathcal{A}_2(\mathcal{A}_1(D)) = t] = \int_{s \in \mathcal{S}} \Pr[\mathcal{A}_1(D) = s] \Pr[\mathcal{A}_2(s) = t] \, ds$ and the logic of the proof is the same. □

In the above proposition, the post-processing algorithm $\mathcal{A}_2$ accesses only the output of $\mathcal{A}_1$ and not the input dataset D. The following proposition applies to the case where $\mathcal{A}_2$ also accesses D.

Proposition 2.3 Sequential composition   *Given $\mathcal{A}_1(\cdot)$ that satisfies ϵ_1-DP, and $\mathcal{A}_2(s, \cdot)$ that satisfies ϵ_2-DP for any s, then $\mathcal{A}(D) = \mathcal{A}_2(\mathcal{A}_1(D), D)$ satisfies $(\epsilon_1 + \epsilon_2)$-DP.*

Proof. Let D and D' be any two neighboring databases. Let $\mathcal{S}$ be $Range(\mathcal{A}_1)$. For any $t \in Range(\mathcal{A}_2)$, we have

$$\Pr[\mathcal{A}_2(\mathcal{A}_1(D), D) = t)] = \sum_{s \in \mathcal{S}} \Pr[\mathcal{A}_1(D) = s] \Pr[\mathcal{A}_2(s, D) = t]$$
$$\leq \sum_{s \in \mathcal{S}} e^{\epsilon_1} \Pr[\mathcal{A}_1(D') = s] e^{\epsilon_2} \Pr[\mathcal{A}_2(s, D') = t]$$
$$= e^{\epsilon_1 + \epsilon_2} \Pr[\mathcal{A}_2(\mathcal{A}_1(D'), D') = t].$$

If $\mathcal{S}$ is not countable, $\Pr[\mathcal{A}_2(\mathcal{A}_1(D), D) = t)] = \int_{s \in \mathcal{S}} \Pr[\mathcal{A}_1(D) = s] \Pr[\mathcal{A}_2(s, D) = t] \, ds$ and the logic of the proof is the same. □

Note that Proposition 2.2 is a special case of Proposition 2.3, where $\mathcal{A}_2$ satisfies 0-DP because it does not look at the input dataset. Proposition 2.3 can be further generalized to the case where there are k such algorithms, each taking two inputs, an auxiliary input consisting of the combined outputs of the previous algorithms, and the input dataset, and satisfying ϵ-DP when the auxiliary input is fixed.

Corollary 2.4 General Sequential Composition   *Let $\mathcal{A}_1, \mathcal{A}_2, \cdots, \mathcal{A}_k$ be k algorithms (that take auxiliary inputs) that satisfy ϵ_1-DP, ϵ_2-DP, $\cdots$, ϵ_k-DP, respectively, with respect to the input dataset. Publishing*

$$\mathbf{t} = \langle t_1, t_2, \cdots, t_k \rangle, \ \text{where} \ t_1 = \mathcal{A}_1(D), t_2 = \mathcal{A}_2(t_1, D), \cdots, t_k = \mathcal{A}_k(\langle t_1, \cdots, t_{k-1} \rangle, D)$$

satisfies $(\sum_{i=1}^{k} \epsilon_i)$-DP.

This follows from Proposition 2.3 via mathematical induction. The ϵ parameter is often referred to as the "**privacy budget**," since it needs to be divided under sequential composition and consumed by individual steps in an algorithm.

2.2.2 PARALLEL COMPOSITION AND CONVEXITY

We now consider another form of composition, where k algorithms are applied to an input dataset D, but each algorithm only to a portion of D. We introduce the notion of a partitioning function. Let $\mathbb{D}$ denote the set of all possible data items. A **partitioning algorithm** f takes an item in $\mathbb{D}$ as input and maps it to a positive integer number. Executing f on D once yields a partitioning of D as follows. One executes f on each element of D, each time resulting in a number. Let k

be the largest number being outputted, then D is partitioned into k partitions, with D_i including all items mapped to i.

Proposition 2.5   Parallel Composition under Unbounded DP.   *Let $\mathcal{A}_1, \mathcal{A}_2, \cdots, \mathcal{A}_k$ be k algorithms that satisfy ϵ_1-DP, ϵ_2-DP, $\cdots$, ϵ_k-DP, respectively. Given a deterministic partitioning function f, let $D_1, D_2, \cdots, D_k$ be the resulting partitions of executing f on D. Publishing $\mathcal{A}_1(D_1), \mathcal{A}_2(D_2), \cdots, \mathcal{A}_k(D_k)$ satisfies $(\max_{i \in [1,...,k]} \epsilon_i)$-DP.*

Proof. Given two neighboring datasets D and D', without loss of generality, assume that D contains one more element than D'. Let the result of partitioning of D and D' be $D_1, D_2, \cdots, D_k$ and $D'_1, D'_2, \cdots, D'_k$, respectively. There exists j such that (1) D_j contains one more element than D'_j, and (2) for any $i \neq j$, $D_i = D'_i$. Denote $\mathcal{A}_1(D_1), \mathcal{A}_2(D_2), \cdots, \mathcal{A}_k(D_k)$ by $\mathcal{A}(D)$. Since these k algorithms run on disjoint sets D_i independently, for any sequence $t = (t_1, t_2, \cdots, t_k)$ of outputs of these k algorithms, where $t_i \in Range(\mathcal{A}_i)$, we have

$$\begin{aligned} \Pr\left[\mathcal{A}(D) = t\right] &= \Pr\left[(\mathcal{A}_1(D_1) = t_1) \wedge (\mathcal{A}_2(D_2) = t_2) \wedge \cdots \wedge (\mathcal{A}_k(D_k) = t_k)\right] \\ &= \Pr\left[\mathcal{A}_j(D_j) = t_j\right] \prod_{i \neq j} \Pr\left[\mathcal{A}_i(D_i) = t_i\right] \\ &\leq e^{\epsilon_j} \Pr\left[\mathcal{A}_j(D'_j) = t_j\right] \prod_{i \neq j} \Pr\left[\mathcal{A}_i(D'_i) = t_i\right] \\ &\leq e^{\max_{i \in [1,...,k]} \epsilon_i} \Pr\left[\mathcal{A}(D') = t\right]. \end{aligned}$$

This proves the proposition.   □

Example 2.6   Publishing histograms based on counts.   Suppose that we have a method to publish the number of records in a set while satisfying ϵ-DP. We can use the parallel composition to turn that method into one for publishing a histogram. A histogram "bins" the range of values, i.e., divides the entire range of values into a series of intervals, and then counts how many values fall into each interval.

Recall that publishing the total number of records in a dataset satisfies 0-DP under the bounded DP interpretation. Thus, if parallel composition were to hold for bounded DP as well, then arbitrary histograms can be published accurately while satisfying 0-DP.

Proposition 2.7   *Parallel composition **does not hold** using the bounded DP interpretation.*

Proof. When one element in a dataset D is replaced by another element to obtain D', after partitioning D and D', we may be in the situation that there exist $i \neq j$ such that D_i contains one additional element than D'_i, and D'_j contains one additional element than D_j. Under bounded DP, $\frac{\Pr[\mathcal{A}_i(D_i)]}{\Pr[\mathcal{A}_i(D'_i)]}$ can be unbounded because D_i and D'_i contain different numbers of elements.   □

Since parallel composition is frequently used to prove that an algorithm satisfies ϵ-DP, Proposition 2.7 suggests that we should use the unbounded interpretation of ϵ-DP wherever possible. If bounded DP is used, one has to be really careful that parallel composition is not used.

Proposition 2.5 is only for the case where the partition function f is deterministic. To prove that it also holds when f is randomized, the following convexity property of DP is helpful.

Proposition 2.8   Convexity   *Given two mechanisms $\mathcal{A}_1$ and $\mathcal{A}_2$ that both satisfy ϵ-DP, and any $p \in [0, 1]$, let $\mathcal{A}$ be the mechanism that applies $\mathcal{A}_1$ with probability p and $\mathcal{A}_2$ with probability $1 - p$. Then $\mathcal{A}$ satisfies ϵ-DP.*

Proof. Let D and D' be any two neighboring databases. For any $t \in Range(\mathcal{A})$, we have

$$
\begin{aligned}
\Pr[\mathcal{A}(D) = t] &= p \Pr[\mathcal{A}_1(D) = t] + (1 - p) \Pr[\mathcal{A}_2(D) = t] \\
&\leq p\, e^\epsilon \Pr[\mathcal{A}_1(D') = t] + (1 - p)\, e^\epsilon \Pr[\mathcal{A}_2(D') = t] \\
&= e^\epsilon \left(p \Pr[\mathcal{A}_1(D') = t] + (1 - p) \Pr[\mathcal{A}_2(D') = t] \right) \\
&= e^\epsilon \Pr[\mathcal{A}(D') = t].
\end{aligned}
$$

The proof is complete.   □

Again, we can generalize the above to the case of k algorithms.

Corollary 2.9   Convexity: General Case   *Given k mechanisms $\mathcal{A}_1, \mathcal{A}_2, \cdots, \mathcal{A}_k$ that satisfy ϵ-DP, and $p_1, p_2, \cdots, p_k \in [0, 1]$ such that $\sum_{i=1}^{k} p_i = 1$, let $\mathcal{A}$ be the mechanism that applies $\mathcal{A}_i$ with probability p_i. Then $\mathcal{A}$ satisfies ϵ-DP.*

This follows from Proposition 2.8 by mathematical induction. With this corollary, we can extend the parallel composition to the case of randomized partition function as well. Note that we require that such a partitioning function f have an upper-bound on the number of partitions it produces, i.e., there exists b such that $\forall x, f(x) \leq b$.

Proposition 2.10   Parallel composition, randomized partition function.   *Let $\mathcal{A}_1, \mathcal{A}_2, \cdots, \mathcal{A}_k$ be k algorithms that satisfy ϵ_1-DP, ϵ_2-DP, $\cdots$, ϵ_k-DP, respectively. Given a possibly randomized partitioning function f, the mechanism of first executing f on D, with $D_1, D_2, \cdots, D_k$ being the resulting partitions, and then publishing $\mathcal{A}_1(D_1), \mathcal{A}_2(D_2), \cdots, \mathcal{A}_k(D_k)$, satisfies $(\max_{i \in [1,...,k]} \epsilon_i)$-DP.*

Proof. Let $\epsilon = \max_{i \in [1,...,k]} \epsilon_i$. We can view the result of f as a probabilistic combination of many deterministic partitioning functions. Consider all possible outputs of f on elements in D. The total number of such combinations is finite. Let f_i be the partitioning function that output the i'th such output, and p_i be the probably that executing f results in output f_i. From Proposition 2.5, the parallel composition under f_i satisfies ϵ-DP. The behavior under f can be viewed as the convex composition of all f_i's, and thus also satisfies ϵ-DP because of Corollary 2.9.   □

2.3   THE LAPLACE MECHANISM

The Laplace mechanism [Dwork et al., 2006] is the first and probably most widely used mechanism for DP. It satisfies ϵ-DP by adding noise to the output of a numerical function. We present first the case where the function outputs a scalar, and then the vector case. We present them separately even though the latter subsumes the former as a special case, because the scalar case is easier to understand.

2.3.1   THE SCALAR CASE

Assume that we have a dataset for patients diagnosed with lung cancer, with one attribute being how many years the patient has been smoking, and another being how many packs of cigarettes the patient smokes on average per day. Suppose that we want to know how many patients have been smoking for more than 15 years, how do we obtain the answer while satisfying ϵ-DP?

In this case, we want to compute $f(D)$, where f outputs a single scalar value. To satisfy ϵ-DP, one can publish $\tilde{f}(D) = f(D) + X$, where X is a random variable drawn from some distribution. What distribution should one use for X? Intuitively, we want the distribution to have 0 as its mean so that $\tilde{f}(D)$ is an unbiased estimate of $f(D)$. Furthermore, we need to ensure that

$$\forall t, \; \frac{\Pr\left[\tilde{f}(D) = t\right]}{\Pr\left[\tilde{f}(D') = t\right]} = \frac{\Pr\left[f(D) + X = t\right]}{\Pr\left[f(D') + X' = t\right]} = \frac{\Pr\left[X = t - f(D)\right]}{\Pr\left[X' = t - f(D')\right]} \leq e^{\epsilon},$$

where X and X' are drawn from the same distribution. Let $d = f(D) - f(D')$; we need to ensure that

$$\forall x, \; \frac{\Pr\left[X = x\right]}{\Pr\left[X' = x + d\right]} \leq e^{\epsilon}. \tag{2.3}$$

We need to ensure that Eq. (2.3) holds for all possible d, and thus need the concept of the global sensitivity of f, which is the maximum change of f between two neighboring datasets D and D'.

Definition 2.11   Global sensitivity.   Let $D \simeq D'$ denote that D and D' are neighboring. The global sensitivity of a function f, denoted by Δ_f, is given below

$$\Delta_f = \max_{D \simeq D'} |f(D) - f(D')|, \tag{2.4}$$

We want to ensure that Eq. (2.3) holds for all $d \leq \Delta_f$. In other words, the probability density function of the noise should have the property that if one moves no more than Δ_f units on the x-axis, the probability should increase or decrease by a factor of no more than e^{ϵ}, i.e., if one moves no more than one unit on the x-axis, the probability should change by a multiplicative factor of no more than e^{ϵ/Δ_f}.

The distribution that naturally satisfies this requirement is $\mathsf{Lap}\left(\frac{\Delta_f}{\epsilon}\right)$, the Laplace distribution, where $\Pr\left[\mathsf{Lap}\left(\beta\right) = x\right] = \frac{1}{2\beta}e^{-|x|/\beta}$. Note that

$$\frac{\Pr\left[\mathsf{Lap}\left(\beta\right) = x\right]}{\Pr\left[\mathsf{Lap}\left(\beta\right) = x + d\right]} \leq e^{d/\beta} \leq e^{\Delta_f/\beta} = e^\epsilon.$$

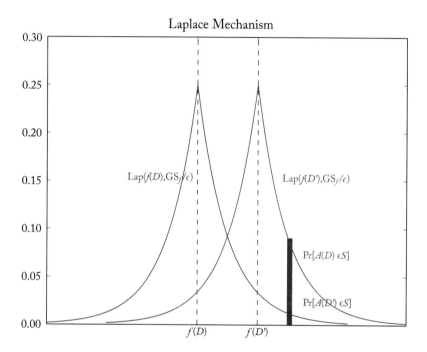

Figure 2.1: Differential privacy via Laplace noise.

Theorem 2.12   Laplace mechanism, scalar case.   *For any function f, the Laplace mechanism* $\mathcal{A}_f(D) = f(D) + \mathsf{Lap}\left(\frac{\Delta_f}{\epsilon}\right)$ *satisfies ϵ-DP.*

Proof. Let X be the noise injected to $f(D)$. So, $X \sim \mathsf{Lap}\left(\frac{\Delta_f}{\epsilon}\right)$.

$$\Pr\left[\mathcal{A}_f(D) = t\right] = \Pr\left[f(D) + X = t\right] = \Pr\left[X = t - f(D)\right] = \frac{\epsilon}{2\Delta_f} \exp\left(\frac{-\epsilon|t - f(D)|}{\Delta_f}\right).$$

Similarly, we have $\Pr\left[\mathcal{A}_f(D') = t\right] = \frac{\epsilon}{2\Delta_f} \exp\left(\frac{-\epsilon|t-f(D')|}{\Delta_f}\right)$. Thus,

$$
\begin{aligned}
\frac{\Pr\left[\mathcal{A}_f(D) = t\right]}{\Pr\left[\mathcal{A}_f(D') = t\right]} &= \frac{\exp\left(\frac{-\epsilon|t - f(D)|}{\Delta_f}\right)}{\exp\left(\frac{-\epsilon|t - f(D')|}{\Delta_f}\right)} \\
&= \exp\left(\frac{\epsilon(|t - f(D')| - |t - f(D)|)}{\Delta_f}\right) \\
&\leq \exp\left(\frac{\epsilon|f(D) - f(D')|}{\Delta_f}\right) \\
&\leq \exp(\epsilon).
\end{aligned}
$$

The first inequality holds because of the triangle inequality with absolute value $|a| - |b| \leq |a - b|$ and the second holds due to Eq. (2.4). $\qquad\square$

Example 2.13   Counting Queries   Queries, such as "how many patients have been smoking for more than 15 years," are counting queries, as they count how many records satisfy a given condition. In general, counting queries have global sensitivity 1, as adding or removing a single record can change the result of a counting query by at most 1. They can thus be answered by the Laplace mechanism with relatively low noise.

Example 2.14   Sum Queries   Queries summing up the values of one attribute for the records that satisfy a given condition have sensitivity that equals the size of the domain of that attribute, and can be answered by the Laplace mechanism.

2.3.2   THE VECTOR CASE

The Laplace mechanism can also be applied to a function f that outputs a vector, in which case, the global sensitivity Δ_f is the maximum L_1 norm of the difference between $f(D)$ and $f(D')$, i.e.:

$$
\Delta_f = \max_{D \simeq D'} ||f(D) - f(D')||_1. \tag{2.5}
$$

And noise calibrated to the global sensitivity should be added to all components of a vector.

Theorem 2.15   Laplace mechanism, the vector case.   *The Laplace mechanism for a function f whose value is a k-dimensional vector, defined below, satisfies ϵ-DP.*

$$
\mathcal{A}_f(D) = f(D) + \langle X_1, X_2, \cdots, X_k \rangle,
$$

where $X_1, X_2, \cdots, X_k$ are i.i.d. random variables drawn from $\mathsf{Lap}\left(\frac{\Delta_f}{\epsilon}\right)$.

Proof. Suppose $f(D) = \langle a_1, a_2, \cdots, a_k \rangle$. For any output $t = \langle t_1, t_2, \cdots, t_k \rangle$,

$$
\begin{aligned}
\Pr\left[\mathcal{A}_f(D) = t\right] &= \Pr\left[f(D) + \langle X_1, X_2, \cdots, X_k \rangle = t\right] \\
&= \Pr\left[(X_1 = t_1 - a_1) \wedge (X_2 = t_2 - a_2) \wedge \cdots \wedge (X_k = t_k - a_k)\right] \\
&= \prod_{i=1}^{k} \Pr\left[X_i = t_i - a_i\right] = \prod_{i=1}^{k} \frac{\epsilon}{2\Delta_f} \exp\left(\frac{-\epsilon|t_i - a_i|}{\Delta_f}\right) \\
&= \left(\frac{\epsilon}{2\Delta_f}\right)^k \exp\left(\frac{-\epsilon \sum_{i=1}^{k} |t_i - a_i|}{\Delta_f}\right) \\
&= \left(\frac{\epsilon}{2\Delta_f}\right)^k \exp\left(\frac{-\epsilon \|t - f(D)\|_1}{\Delta_f}\right)
\end{aligned}
$$

Similarly, $\Pr\left[\mathcal{A}_f(D') = t\right] = \left(\frac{\epsilon}{2\Delta_f}\right)^k \exp\left(\frac{-\epsilon \|t - f(D')\|_1}{\Delta_f}\right)$. Thus,

$$
\begin{aligned}
\frac{\Pr\left[\mathcal{A}_f(D) = t\right]}{\Pr\left[\mathcal{A}_f(D') = t\right]} &= \frac{\exp\left(\frac{-\epsilon \|t - f(D)\|_1}{\Delta_f}\right)}{\exp\left(\frac{-\epsilon \|t - f(D')\|_1}{\Delta_f}\right)} \\
&= \exp\left(\frac{\epsilon(\|t - f(D')\|_1 - \|t - f(D)\|_1)}{\Delta_f}\right) \\
&\leq \exp\left(\frac{\epsilon \|f(D) - f(D')\|_1}{\Delta_f}\right) \\
&\leq \exp(\epsilon).
\end{aligned}
$$

The first inequality holds because of the triangle inequality for the L_1-norm and the second holds due to Eq. (2.5). □

Example 2.16 Histogram   Consider again the dataset for patients diagnosed with lung cancer, with one attribute being how many years the patient has been smoking, and another being how many packs of cigarettes the patient smokes on average per day. We can publish a one-dimensional histogram that counts how many patients have been smoking for a certain number of years, where the number of years is divided into a few bins, such as $\{[0-4], [5-9], [10-14], [15-19], [20-29], [30+]\}$. Publishing such a histogram has global sensitivity 1, since adding or removing one patient changes only the count of one bin by 1. Thus publishing a noisy histogram with noise drawn from the distribution $\mathsf{Lap}\left(\frac{1}{\epsilon}\right)$ added to each bin count satisfies ϵ-DP.

Similarly, we can publish a two-dimensional histogram that also considers how many packs of cigarettes a patient smokes on average per day. The same Laplace mechanism would apply. Note that to satisfy ϵ-DP, it is important that the way the attribute values are partitioned into bins does not depend on the input dataset. If the partitioning depends on the input dataset, one has to ensure that the partitioning and the histogram together satisfy ϵ-DP, using composition properties in Section 2.2.

Note that the above noisy Histogram method can be viewed either as applying the Laplace mechanism with a vector output, or as a parallel composition of the counting function.

2.4 THE EXPONENTIAL MECHANISM

While the Laplace mechanism provides a solution to handle numeric queries, it cannot be applied to non-numeric valued queries. This motivates the development of the exponential mechanism [McSherry and Talwar, 2007], which can be applied whether a function's output is numerical or categorical.

Suppose that one wants to publish $f(D)$, and let O denote the set of possible outputs. To satisfy ϵ-DP, a mechanism should output values in O following some probability distribution. Naturally, some values in O are more desirable than others. For example, the most desirable output is the true value $f(D)$, and one has natural preferences among other values as well. For example, consider a transactional dataset D, and one wants to output the item that appears most frequently in D. Then O is the set of all items, and between two items, we prefer to output the one that appears more often. This preference is encoded using a quality function $q : (\mathbb{D} \times O) \to \mathbb{R}$, where $\mathbb{D}$ denotes the set of all datasets, and $\mathbb{R}$ denotes the set of all real numbers. Without loss of generality, we assume that a higher quality value indicates better utility. For example, in the most frequent item case, a natural choice is to define $q(D, o)$ to be the number of times the item o appears in D.

2.4.1 THE GENERAL CASE OF THE EXPONENTIAL MECHANISM

Definition 2.17 The Exponential Mechanism.   For any quality function $q : (\mathbb{D} \times O) \to \mathbb{R}$, and a privacy parameter ϵ, the exponential mechanism $\mathcal{M}_q^\epsilon(D)$ outputs $o \in O$ with probability proportional to $\exp\left(\frac{\epsilon q(D,o)}{2\Delta q}\right)$, where

$$\Delta q = \max_{\forall o, D \simeq D'} |q(D, o) - q(D', o)|$$

is the sensitivity of the quality function. That is,

$$\Pr\left[\mathcal{M}_q^\epsilon(D) = o\right] = \frac{\exp\left(\frac{\epsilon q(D,o)}{2\Delta q}\right)}{\sum_{o' \in O} \exp\left(\frac{\epsilon q(D,o')}{2\Delta q}\right)}.$$

Theorem 2.18 The Exponential Mechanism.   *The exponential mechanism satisfies ϵ-differential privacy.*

Proof. For any two neighboring datasets D and D' and any $o \in O$,

$$\frac{\exp\left(\frac{\epsilon q(D,o)}{2\Delta q}\right)}{\exp\left(\frac{\epsilon q(D',o)}{2\Delta q}\right)} = \exp\left(\frac{\epsilon(q(D,o) - q(D',o))}{2\Delta q}\right) \leq \exp\left(\frac{\epsilon}{2}\right), \tag{2.6}$$

Because of the symmetry of neighboring, we also have $\forall o'$, $\exp\left(\frac{\epsilon q(D',o')}{2\Delta q}\right) \leq \exp\left(\frac{\epsilon}{2}\right) \exp\left(\frac{\epsilon q(D,o')}{2\Delta q}\right)$.

Now we prove ϵ-DP of the exponential mechanism. For any output o of $\mathcal{M}_q^\epsilon$,

$$
\begin{aligned}
\frac{\Pr\left[\mathcal{M}_q^\epsilon(D) = o\right]}{\Pr\left[\mathcal{M}_q^\epsilon(D') = o\right]} &= \frac{\frac{\exp\left(\frac{\epsilon q(D,o)}{2\Delta q}\right)}{\sum_{o' \in O} \exp\left(\frac{\epsilon q(D,o')}{2\Delta q}\right)}}{\frac{\exp\left(\frac{\epsilon q(D',o)}{2\Delta q}\right)}{\sum_{o' \in O} \exp\left(\frac{\epsilon q(D',o')}{2\Delta q}\right)}} \\
&= \left(\frac{\exp\left(\frac{\epsilon q(D,o)}{2\Delta q}\right)}{\exp\left(\frac{\epsilon q(D',o)}{2\Delta q}\right)}\right) \cdot \left(\frac{\sum_{o' \in O} \exp\left(\frac{\epsilon q(D',o')}{2\Delta q}\right)}{\sum_{o' \in O} \exp\left(\frac{\epsilon q(D,o')}{2\Delta q}\right)}\right) \\
&\leq \exp\left(\frac{\epsilon}{2}\right) \cdot \left(\frac{\sum_{o' \in O} \exp\left(\frac{\epsilon}{2}\right) \exp\left(\frac{\epsilon q(D,o')}{2\Delta q}\right)}{\sum_{o' \in O} \exp\left(\frac{\epsilon q(D,o')}{2\Delta q}\right)}\right) \\
&\leq \exp\left(\frac{\epsilon}{2}\right) \cdot \exp\left(\frac{\epsilon}{2}\right) \left(\frac{\sum_{o' \in O} \exp\left(\frac{\epsilon q(D,o')}{2\Delta q}\right)}{\sum_{o' \in O} \exp\left(\frac{\epsilon q(D,o')}{2\Delta q}\right)}\right) \\
&= \exp(\epsilon).
\end{aligned}
\tag{2.7}
$$

$\square$

2.4.2   THE MONOTONIC CASE OF THE EXPONENTIAL MECHANISM

In some usages of the exponential mechanism, the quality function $q(D,o)$ is monotonic in the sense that for any D and D' that are neighboring, either $\forall o \in O$, $q(D,o) \geq q(D',o)$, or $\forall o \in O$, $q(D,o) \leq q(D',o)$. This is generally the case when the quality function is based on counting the number of records satisfying some condition. For example, this is the case when applying the exponential mechanism to frequent itemsets mining. For such quality functions, the effectiveness of the exponential mechanism can be improved. One can make more accurate selections by choosing each possible output with probability proportional to $\exp(\frac{\epsilon q(D,t)}{\Delta q})$, instead of $\exp(\frac{\epsilon q(D,t)}{2\Delta q})$. To see that doing so satisfies ϵ-DP, observe that Eq. (2.7) of the proof is a product of two terms, and for a monotonic quality function, whenever the first term is ≥ 1, the second term is ≤ 1; thus upper-bounding the first term by e^ϵ suffices. See below for details.

The utility benefit of doing this is equivalent to doubling the privacy budget ϵ. Suppose that under the general exponential mechanism, the odds of choosing the best option relative to another less preferable one is 10 : 1, then under the monotonic exponential mechanism, the odds become 100 : 1.

Corollary 2.19   *For any monotonic quality function* $q : (\mathbb{D} \times O) \to \mathbb{R}$ *and a privacy parameter* ϵ, *the exponential mechanism* $\mathcal{M}_q^\epsilon(D)$ *outputting* $o \in O$ *with probability proportional to* $e^{\epsilon q(D,o)/(\Delta q)}$ *satisfies* ϵ-*DP.*

Proof. Let D and D' be two neighboring datasets. Without loss of generality, assume $D' = D \cup \{r\}$, and the quality function $q(D, o)$ is monotonically increasing when the size of a dataset increases. So, for any output $o' \in O$,

$$\exp\left(\frac{\epsilon q(D, o')}{\Delta q}\right) \leq \exp\left(\frac{\epsilon q(D', o')}{\Delta q}\right).$$

Similarly to Eq.(2.6), we have

$$\exp\left(\frac{\epsilon q(D', o')}{\Delta q}\right) \leq \exp(\epsilon) \exp\left(\frac{\epsilon q(D, o')}{\Delta q}\right).$$

Now we turn to the privacy proof of the exponential mechanism in the same way as the proof above.

On one hand, we observe that

$$\frac{\Pr\left[\mathcal{M}_q^\epsilon(D) = o\right]}{\Pr\left[\mathcal{M}_q^\epsilon(D') = o\right]} = \left(\frac{\exp\left(\frac{\epsilon q(D,o)}{\Delta q}\right)}{\exp\left(\frac{\epsilon q(D',o)}{\Delta q}\right)}\right) \cdot \left(\frac{\sum_{o' \in O} \exp\left(\frac{\epsilon q(D',o')}{\Delta q}\right)}{\sum_{o' \in O} \exp\left(\frac{\epsilon q(D,o')}{\Delta q}\right)}\right)$$

$$\leq 1 \cdot \exp(\epsilon) \left(\frac{\sum_{o' \in O} \exp\left(\frac{\epsilon q(D,o')}{\Delta q}\right)}{\sum_{o' \in O} \exp\left(\frac{\epsilon q(D,o')}{\Delta q}\right)}\right) = \exp(\epsilon).$$

On the other hand,

$$\frac{\Pr\left[\mathcal{M}_q^\epsilon(D') = o\right]}{\Pr\left[\mathcal{M}_q^\epsilon(D) = o\right]} = \left(\frac{\exp\left(\frac{\epsilon q(D',o)}{\Delta q}\right)}{\exp\left(\frac{\epsilon q(D,o)}{\Delta q}\right)}\right) \cdot \left(\frac{\sum_{o' \in O} \exp\left(\frac{\epsilon q(D,o')}{\Delta q}\right)}{\sum_{o' \in O} \exp\left(\frac{\epsilon q(D',o')}{\Delta q}\right)}\right)$$

$$\leq \exp(\epsilon) \cdot 1 = \exp(\epsilon).$$

In summary, $e^{-\epsilon} \leq \frac{\Pr[\mathcal{M}_q^\epsilon(D)=o]}{\Pr[\mathcal{M}_q^\epsilon(D')=o]} \leq e^\epsilon$ and thus the corollary holds. $\square$

2.4.3   CASE STUDY: COMPUTING MODE AND MEDIAN

Mode and median are common statistical quantities, and we use them to illustrate the application of the exponential mechanism. Given a set of numbers in a well-defined range, e.g., incomes of individuals as integers in the range between 0 and 1,000,000, how to compute the mode and how to compute the median?

We note that the Laplace mechanism is ineffective here. The global sensitivity for the median function is $\frac{1,000,000-0}{2} =$500,000. Consider a dataset with n values of 0 and n values of 1,000,000; the median is 500,000. However, adding an additional value of 0 changes the median to 0. Using the Laplace mechanism, if $\epsilon \leq 1$, the accuracy of the output is a little better than randomly sampling a point in the data domain.

Applying the Laplace mechanism to the mode problem is likely to result in a floating point number, even when the input dataset consists of only integers. One can ensure that only integer values can be outputted either by using a post-processing step that converts floating point numbers to integers, or directly using a discrete exponential distribution similar to the Laplace distribution. However, it remains that the output of such a noisy model method is likely to be a value that does not even appear in the input dataset.

Example 2.20   Finding Mode via Exponential Mechanism   Let each integer from 0 to 1,000,000 be a possible output. We choose the quality of outputting x to be $n_{=x}$, which gives the number of data points equal to x. The sensitivity of the quality function is 1, and the quality function is monotonic. Thus, the probability that x is being outputted is

$$\frac{\exp\left(\epsilon\, n_{=x}\right)}{\sum_{y=0}^{1,000,000} \exp\left(\epsilon\, n_{=x}\right)}.$$

When the number of times the true mode appears is more than $c\,\frac{\ln(1,000,000)}{\epsilon}$, for some small constant of c (perhaps around 5), then with high probability either the true mode, or some value that also appears similarly frequently, will be outputted.

Example 2.21   Finding Median via Exponential Mechanism   Let each integer from 0 to 1,000,000 be a possible output. We choose the quality of outputting x to be $-\min_{n_{<x} \leq j \leq n_{<x+1}} |j - n/2|$, where $n_{<x}$ gives the number of data points less than x, respectively. The sensitivity of the quality function is $1/2$. Adding an item increases n by $1/2$, and j either remains unchanged, or increases by 1. This quality function, however, is not monotonic.

Alternatively, we can divide the total range $[0 \ldots 1,000,000]$ into m equal-size ranges, and define the quality of selecting each range $[v_i, v_{j+1})$ to be $-\min_{n_{<v_i} \leq j \leq n_{<v_{j+1}}} |j - n/2|$. After a range is selected via the exponential mechanism, we can select a point in the range at uniform random.

We note that a similar method can be used to find the k'th item. By finding the value corresponding to the 25'th percentile and the 75'th percentile, one can then compute the interquartile range (IQR).

2.4.4   DISCUSSION ON THE EXPONENTIAL MECHANISM

When applying the exponential mechanism, the probability that a low-quality output is selected is exponentially smaller than that of a high-quality output. However, when the number of low-quality outputs is exponentially more than the number of high-quality outputs, the accuracy suffers.

In McSherry and Talwar [2007], it is observed that the Laplace mechanism can be viewed as a special case of the exponential mechanism, by using the quality function for each output o to be $q(D, o) = -|f(D) - o|$. The global sensitivity of this quality function is the same as the global sensitivity of the function f.

$$
\begin{aligned}
\Delta q &= \max_{o,D,D'} |q(D,o) - q(D',o)| \\
&= \max_{o,D,D'} ||f(D') - o| - |f(D) - o|| \\
&= \max_{D,D'} |f(D) - f(D')| \\
&= \Delta_f
\end{aligned}
$$

We note, however, that such a quality function is not monotonic, and the probability of outputting a value o is proportional to $\exp\left(\frac{-\epsilon|f(D)-o|}{2\Delta_f}\right)$. This is different from the Laplace mechanism, where the probability of outputting a value o is proportional to $\exp\left(\frac{-\epsilon|f(D)-o|}{\Delta_f}\right)$. Thus, the Laplace mechanism is more accurate than using the exponential mechanism this way. In the exponential mechanism, a value at distance r away from the true answer $f(D)$ will be selected with a probability that is $\exp\left(\frac{-r\epsilon}{2\Delta_f}\right)$ of the probability that $f(D)$ is selected. In the Laplace mechanism, a value at distance r away will be selected with a probability that is $\exp\left(\frac{-r\epsilon}{\Delta_f}\right)$ of the probability that $f(D)$ is selected.

Similarly, McSherry and Talwar [2007] observed that technically the exponential mechanism can capture any differentially privacy mechanism $\mathcal{A}$ by taking $q(D, o)$ to be the logarithm of the probability density of $\mathcal{A}(D)$ at o. Thus the exponential mechanism has "captured the full class of differential privacy mechanisms." Since $\mathcal{A}$ satisfies ϵ-DP, this ensures that the sensitivity of such a quality function is ϵ. Again, applying the exponential mechanism thus obtained from $\mathcal{A}$ will lead to a mechanism that is different from (and generally slightly worse than) $\mathcal{A}$, because the resulting quality function is not monotonic, and the exponential mechanism will output o that is proportional to $\exp\left(\frac{q(D,o)}{2}\right)$ instead of $\exp(q(D, o))$, as in the original mechanism.

Thus the argument in McSherry and Talwar [2007] that the exponential mechanism can capture any differentially private mechanism is incorrect. It is an intriguing open question whether it is true that the exponential mechanism can capture every differentially private mechanism. That is, the question is whether for any algorithm $\mathcal{A}$ that satisfies ϵ-DP, there exists a quality function such that applying the quality function in the exponential mechanism results in an algorithm equivalent to $\mathcal{A}$. Our conjecture is that the answer to this question is "no."

We point out that it is true that the exponential mechanism is very versatile and can be broadly applied. To use the exponential mechanism effectively, one needs two things. The first is a way to narrow down the set of possible outputs to a set that is not very big. The second is to design a quality function that both has low sensitivity and at the same time effectively separates the more desired outcomes from the less desired ones. These can become quite challenging at times. Almost all effective private algorithms use combinations of Laplace and exponential mechanisms.

2.5   CASE STUDY: COMPUTING AVERAGE

We now use a case study to further illustrate the different methods for satisfying DP. We show that the same problem can be solved by different methods. We also show that subtle differences in an algorithm can cause an algorithm to be no longer private. Also some small changes can improve the utility of an algorithm by reducing a constant factor. The treatment may appear tedious; this is because this is the first relatively complicated example problem, so we keep a lot of details. We also want to illustrate subtleties that can exist. Readers can safely skip this section.

Consider the following query: "On average how many packs of cigarettes do patients who have been smoking for more than 15 years smoke?" This asks the average value of one attribute for records that satisfy a certain condition. This is an important primitive that is useful in many contexts. We now explore ways to answer the average query.

More formally, we have as input D the input dataset, c a selection condition, an attribute a taking values in the range $[a_{\min}, a_{\max}]$. Let $\Delta_a = a_{\max} - a_{\min}$, x_a to denote the element x's value in attribute a, and $\sigma_c(D)$ to denote the set of all elements in D satisfying the condition c. We want to compute the following function:

$$\mathsf{Avg}_c^a(D) = \begin{cases} \frac{\sum_{x \in \sigma_c(D)} x_a}{|\sigma_c(D)|} & \text{when } \sigma_c(D) \neq \emptyset \\ \frac{a_{\min} + a_{\max}}{2} & \text{when } \sigma_c(D) = \emptyset \end{cases} \tag{2.8}$$

2.5.1   APPLYING THE LAPLACE AND THE EXPONENTIAL MECHANISM

One straightforward way to answer the average query is to inject Laplace noise with scale proportional to the global sensitivity of the average query. The global sensitivity of $\mathsf{Avg}_c^a(D)$ defined in Eq. (2.8) is $|\frac{a_{\max} - a_{\min}}{2}|$, which is very high. Such a direct application of the Laplace mechanism has poor accuracy because it is adding noises sufficient for the worst-case scenarios where very few data points satisfy the condition, and thus the average is greatly influenced by adding or removing a single data point.

We can also use the exponential mechanism for the average query, similar to that for mode and median. A natural choice for the quality function is as follows: the quality for outputting o is defined to be $-|\sum_{x \in \sigma_c(D)}(x_a - o)|$. Thus the true average avg has a quality of 0, and any other value o has the quality $-|\sigma_c(D)| * |o - avg|$. The sensitivity of the quality function is $\Delta_a = a_{\max} - a_{\min}$, since in the worst case adding a new value $a_{\max}$ would change the quality for $o = a_{\min}$ by Δ_a. We note that this quality function is not monotonic, and the general exponential mechanism is needed. When $|\sigma_c(D)|$ is large, any value o that is not very close to avg has very low probability of being selected.

2.5.2   APPLYING THE LAPLACE MECHANISM AND COMPOSITION

Another way to answer the average query is to use the sequential composition property (2.3) and issue a count query and a sum query, answering each with the Laplace mechanism. One has to divide the privacy budget ϵ for these two queries. This way is shown in Algorithm 2.1. For simplicity, we assume that D, the input to the algorithm, is the set of a values for elements in input dataset D satisfying condition c; thus D is simply a one-dimensional dataset.

Algorithm 2.1 NoisyAverage: Simple Laplace

Input: D: one dimensional dataset, ϵ: privacy parameter, $[a_{\min}, a_{\max}]$: data range

$\tilde{S} \leftarrow D.Sum() + \mathsf{Lap}(2(a_{\max} - a_{\min})/\epsilon)$
$\tilde{C} \leftarrow D.Count() + \mathsf{Lap}(2/\epsilon)$
if $\tilde{C} \leq 1$ **then**
    return $\frac{a_{\min} + a_{\max}}{2}$
else
    return $\frac{\tilde{S}}{\tilde{C}}$
end if

To see that Algorithm 2.1 satisfies ϵ-DP, observe that computing $\tilde{S}$ and $\tilde{C}$ each satisfies $(\epsilon/2)$-DP. After these are computed, the rest of the algorithm does not access the input dataset and does not affect privacy according to Proposition 2.2.

2.5.3   A NON-PRIVATE AVERAGE ALGORITHM USING ACCURATE COUNT

An intriguing question is whether average can be computed without adding noise to the count. After all, we are not actually outputting the count. Only the noisy average is outputted. Consider the following noisy average algorithm:

$$\mathsf{NAvg}_c^a(D) = \begin{cases} \frac{(\sum_{x \in \sigma_c(D)} x_a) + \mathsf{Lap}(\frac{\Delta a}{\epsilon})}{|\sigma_c(D)|} & \text{when } \sigma_c(D) \neq \emptyset \\ \mathsf{Uniform}([a_{\min}, a_{\max}]) & \text{when } \sigma_c(D) = \emptyset \end{cases} \tag{2.9}$$

Does the above satisfy ϵ-DP? For neighboring D and D', without loss of generality, assume that $\sigma_c(D)$ contains one more record than $\sigma_c(D')$ and the record has value a'. Let $n = |\sigma_c(D')|$ and then $|\sigma_c(D)| = n + 1$. Let X be a random variable that follows the distribution $\mathsf{Lap}\left(\frac{\Delta a}{\epsilon}\right)$. For any output value z, we have:

$$\frac{\Pr\left[NAvg_c^a(D) = z\right]}{\Pr\left[NAvg_c^a(D') = z\right]} = \frac{\Pr\left[\left(X + \sum_{x \in \sigma_c(D)} x_a\right)/(n+1) = z\right]}{\Pr\left[\left(X + \sum_{x \in \sigma_c(D')} x_a\right)/n = z\right]}$$

$$= \frac{\Pr\left[X = zn - \left(\sum_{x \in \sigma_c(D')} x_a\right) + z - a'\right]}{\Pr\left[X = zn - \left(\sum_{x \in \sigma_c(D')} x_a\right)\right]}$$

$$= e^{z-a'}.$$

Since z is unbounded, $z - a'$ could be arbitrarily large, and thus the mechanism does not satisfy ϵ-DP. However, we know that the true average must be in the range $[a_{min}, a_{max}]$; if we restrict the output to be in that range, we can ensure that $|z - a'| \leq \Delta_a$, then we have the desired inequality. This naturally leads to the technique of "clamping down" on the output of the mechanism to require that $Avg_c^a(D)$'s output is always within $[a_{min}, a_{max}]$. It might appear that this yields a method for computing average. Indeed, the PINQ system [McSherry] uses the following algorithm (Algorithm 2.2) for computing noisy average.

Algorithm 2.2 NoisyAverage Resampling (from [McSherry])

Input: D : one dimensional dataset, ϵ: privacy parameter, $[a_{min}, a_{max}]$: data range

   $S \leftarrow D.Sum()$
   $C \leftarrow D.Count()$
   if $C = 0$ **then**
      return $Uniform(a_{min}, a_{max})$
   end if
   $A \leftarrow \frac{S + \text{Lap}((a_{max} - a_{min})/\epsilon)}{C}$
   while $A < a_{min}$ or $A > a_{max}$ **do**
      $A \leftarrow \frac{S + \text{Lap}(((a_{max} - a_{min}))/\epsilon)}{C}$
   end while
   return A

Unfortunately, the above algorithm (Algorithm 2.2) does not satisfy ϵ-DP. In this algorithm, the true count is used. When the noisy average is out of the range $[a_{min}, a_{max}]$, it keeps resampling until the noisy average falls into this range. This has the effect of scaling up the probability that the algorithm outputs o for each value $o \in [a_{min}, a_{max}]$. The multiplicative factor for scaling up is 1 over the total probability density that adding Laplace noise causes the noisy average to fall within the range $[a_{min}, a_{max}]$. However, when two neighboring datasets have different averages, the total densities differ, resulting in different scaling factors being used. This difference is affected by the range as well as ϵ.

For a counter example, consider $D = \{-1\}$, $D' = \{-1, 1\}$, and $a_{max} = 1$, $a_{min} = -1$. Let $X \sim \text{Lap}(2/\epsilon)$ denote the Laplace noise injected to the sum queries. Let $\mathcal{A}$ be the algorithm. For dataset D, the true average is -1; thus when $X = 0$, it will output 0.

$$\Pr[\mathcal{A}(D) = -1] = \Pr[X = 0 | X \in [0, 2]]$$
$$= \frac{\frac{\epsilon}{4} \exp\left(-\frac{\epsilon}{2}|0|\right)}{\int_0^2 \frac{\epsilon}{4} \exp\left(-\frac{\epsilon}{2}|x|\right) dx} = \frac{\frac{\epsilon}{4}}{\frac{1-\exp(-\epsilon)}{2}}$$
$$= \frac{\epsilon}{2(1 - \exp(-\epsilon))}.$$

For D', the true average is 0, and the noise added to the true average is $\frac{X}{2}$, since D' has two elements. Thus when $X = -2$, it will output -1.

$$\Pr\left[\mathcal{A}(D') = -1\right] = \Pr[X = -2 | X \in [-2, 2]]$$
$$= \frac{\frac{\epsilon}{4} \exp\left(-\frac{\epsilon}{2}|-2|\right)}{\int_{-2}^2 \frac{\epsilon}{4} \exp\left(-\frac{\epsilon}{2}|x|\right) dx} = \frac{\frac{\epsilon \exp(-\epsilon)}{4}}{1 - \exp(-\epsilon)}$$
$$= \frac{\epsilon \exp(-\epsilon)}{4(1 - \exp(-\epsilon))}.$$

Therefore,

$$\frac{\Pr[\mathcal{A}(D) = -1]}{\Pr[\mathcal{A}(D') = -1]} = \frac{\frac{\epsilon}{2(1-\exp(-\epsilon))}}{\frac{\epsilon \exp(-\epsilon)}{4(1-\exp(-\epsilon))}} = 2\exp(\epsilon) > \exp(\epsilon)!$$

2.5.4   NOISYAVERAGE WITH ACCURATE COUNT

It turns out that using a different clamping-down method from Algorithm 2.2 would remedy the problem of non-privacy. Instead of re-sampling the random noise until the result is within the range, one can limit the output to be in the desired range, denoted by $\Pi_{[a_{min}, a_{max}]}(\cdot)$. That is,

$$\Pi_{[a_{min}, a_{max}]}(y) = \begin{cases} a_{min}, & \text{when } y < a_{min} \\ y, & \text{when } a_{min} \leq y \leq a_{max} \\ a_{max}, & \text{when } y > a_{max} \end{cases}$$

However, after doing this, the probability distribution is discrete at points a_{min} and a_{max} and continuous between them. We must also change how to return an answer when there is no element that satisfies the condition, in order to satisfy ϵ-DP. This leads to Algorithm 2.3.

Proposition 2.22   *Algorithm 2.3 satisfies ϵ-DP.* This proof is quite long and tedious. We include the proof because to our knowledge this algorithm has not been presented in the literature before. Feel free to skip this proof when reading.

Algorithm 2.3 NoisyAverage Clamping-Down

Input: D: one dimensional dataset, ϵ: privacy parameter, $[a_{\min}, a_{\max}]$: data range

    $S \leftarrow D.Sum()$

    $C \leftarrow D.Count()$

    if $C = 0$ **then**

        return $a_{\min}$ with prob $\frac{1}{2}\exp(-\epsilon/2)$, $a_{\max}$ with prob $\frac{1}{2}\exp(-\epsilon/2)$, and a value sampled uniformly from $[a_{\min}, a_{\max}]$ with prob $1 - \exp(-\epsilon/2)$

    end if

    $A \leftarrow \left(\frac{S + \mathrm{Lap}((a_{\max} - a_{\min})/\epsilon)}{C} \right)$

    if $A < a_{\min}$ **then**

        return $a_{\min}$

    else if $A > a_{\max}$ **then**

        return $a_{\max}$

    else

        return A

    end if

Proof. For neighboring D and D', when $\sigma_c(D) = \sigma_c(D')$, we have $\forall z$, $\Pr\left[\mathsf{Avg}_c^a(D) = z\right] = \Pr\left[\mathsf{Avg}_c^a(D') = z\right]$. Otherwise, without loss of generality, assume that $\sigma_c(D)$ contains one more record than $\sigma_c(D')$ and the record has value a'. Let $n = |\sigma_c(D')|$ and then $|\sigma_c(D)| = n + 1$. Let X be a random variable that follows the distribution $\mathsf{Lap}\left(\frac{\Delta_a}{\epsilon}\right)$ and z be an output.

    Case 1: $\sigma_c(D') \neq \emptyset$. For any output value z such that $a_{\min} < z < a_{\max}$, we have:

$$
\frac{\Pr\left[\mathsf{Avg}_c^a(D) = z\right]}{\Pr\left[\mathsf{Avg}_c^a(D') = z\right]} = \frac{\Pr\left[\left(X + \sum_{x \in \sigma_c(D)} x_a\right)/(n+1) = z\right]}{\Pr\left[\left(X + \sum_{x \in \sigma_c(D')} x_a\right)/n = z\right]}
$$

$$
= \frac{\Pr\left[X = zn + z - \sum_{x \in \sigma_c(D')} x_a - a'\right]}{\Pr\left[X = zn - \sum_{x \in \sigma_c(D')} x_a\right]}
$$

$$
= \frac{\exp\left(-\frac{\epsilon}{\Delta_a}\left|zn - \sum_{x \in \sigma_c(D')} x_a + (z - a')\right|\right)}{\exp\left(-\frac{\epsilon}{\Delta_a}\left|zn - \sum_{x \in \sigma_c(D')} x_a\right|\right)}
$$

$$
\in [e^{-\epsilon}, e^{\epsilon}].
$$

The last expression holds because $|z - a'| \leq a_{\max} - a_{\min} = \Delta_a$. When $z = a_{\min}$, we have

$$\Pr\left[\text{Avg}_c^a(D) = a_{\min}\right] = \Pr\left[\frac{\sum_{x \in \sigma_c(D)} x_a + X}{n + 1} < a_{\min}\right]$$

$$= \int_{-\infty}^{a_{\min}} f_Y(y) dy,$$

where $f_Y(y)$ is the probability density function of the random variable $Y = \frac{\sum_{x \in \sigma_c(D)} x_a + X}{n+1}$, a function of a Laplace random variable. Using the change-of-variable technique, the probability density function of Y is:

$$f_Y(y) = (n + 1)\frac{\epsilon}{2\Delta_a} \exp\left(-\frac{\epsilon \left|(n + 1)y - \sum_{x \in \sigma_c(D)} x_a\right|}{\Delta_a}\right).$$

So,

$$\Pr\left[\text{Avg}_c^a(D) = a_{\min}\right] = \int_{-\infty}^{a_{\min}} (n + 1)\frac{\epsilon}{2\Delta_a} \exp\left(-\frac{\epsilon \left|(n + 1)y - \sum_{x \in \sigma_c(D)} x_a\right|}{\Delta_a}\right) dy$$

$$= \int_{-\infty}^{a_{\min}} (n + 1)\frac{\epsilon}{2\Delta_a} \exp\left(\frac{\epsilon \left((n + 1)y - \sum_{x \in \sigma_c(D)} x_a\right)}{\Delta_a}\right) dy$$

$$= \frac{1}{2} \int_{-\infty}^{a_{\min}} \exp\left(\frac{\epsilon \left((n + 1)y - \sum_{x \in \sigma_c(D)} x_a\right)}{\Delta_a}\right) d$$

$$\left(\frac{\epsilon \left((n + 1)y - \sum_{x \in \sigma_c(D)} x_a\right)}{\Delta_a}\right)$$

$$= \frac{1}{2} \exp\left(\frac{\epsilon \left((n + 1)a_{\min} - \sum_{x \in \sigma_c(D)} x_a\right)}{\Delta_a}\right)$$

where the second equality holds because $y \leq x_a$ for any $x \in \sigma_c(D)$ since $y \leq a_{\min}$.

Similarly,

$$\Pr\left[\text{Avg}_c^a(D') = a_{\min}\right] = \frac{1}{2} \exp\left(\frac{\epsilon \left(n a_{\min} - \sum_{x \in \sigma_c(D')} x_a\right)}{\Delta_a}\right).$$

Therefore, the ratio

$$\frac{\Pr\left[\mathsf{Avg}_c^a(D) = a_{\min}\right]}{\Pr\left[\mathsf{Avg}_c^a(D') = a_{\min}\right]} = \frac{\exp\left(\frac{\epsilon\left((n+1)a_{\min}-\sum_{x\in\sigma_c(D)}x_a\right)}{\Delta_a}\right)}{\exp\left(\frac{\epsilon\left(na_{\min}-\sum_{x\in\sigma_c(D')}x_a\right)}{\Delta_a}\right)}$$

$$= \exp\left(\frac{\epsilon(a_{\min}-a')}{\Delta_a}\right).$$

So the ratio $e^{-\epsilon} \le \dfrac{\Pr\left[\mathsf{Avg}_c^a(D)=a_{\min}\right]}{\Pr\left[\mathsf{Avg}_c^a(D')=a_{\min}\right]} \le 1 < e^{\epsilon}$ because $a' \in [a_{\min}, a_{\max}]$.

When $z = a_{\max}$,

$$\Pr\left[\mathsf{Avg}_c^a(D) = a_{\max}\right] = \Pr\left[\frac{\sum_{x\in\sigma_c(D)} x_a + Lap(\frac{\Delta_a}{\epsilon})}{n+1} > a_{\max}\right]$$

$$= \int_{a_{\max}}^{\infty} (n+1)\frac{\epsilon}{2\Delta_a} \exp\left(-\frac{\epsilon\left|(n+1)y - \sum_{x\in\sigma_c(D)}x_a\right|}{\Delta_a}\right) dy$$

$$= \int_{a_{\max}}^{\infty} (n+1)\frac{\epsilon}{2\Delta_a} \exp\left(-\frac{\epsilon\left((n+1)y - \sum_{x\in\sigma_c(D)}x_a\right)}{\Delta_a}\right) dy$$

$$= \frac{1}{2}\exp\left(\frac{-\epsilon\left((n+1)a_{\max} - \sum_{x\in\sigma_c(D)}x_a\right)}{\Delta_a}\right).$$

Similarly,

$$\Pr\left[\mathsf{Avg}_c^a(D) = a_{\max}\right] = \frac{1}{2}\exp\left(\frac{-\epsilon\left(na_{\max} - \sum_{x\in\sigma_c(D')}x_a\right)}{\Delta_a}\right).$$

So the ratio

$$\frac{\Pr\left[\mathsf{Avg}_c^a(D) = a_{\max}\right]}{\Pr\left[\mathsf{Avg}_c^a(D') = a_{\max}\right]} = \frac{\exp\left(\frac{-\epsilon\left((n+1)a_{\max}-\sum_{x\in\sigma_c(D)}x_a\right)}{\Delta_a}\right)}{\exp\left(\frac{-\epsilon\left(na_{\max}-\sum_{x\in\sigma_c(D')}x_a\right)}{\Delta_a}\right)}$$

$$= \exp\left(\frac{-\epsilon(a_{\max}-a')}{\Delta_a}\right),$$

which means $e^{-\epsilon} \le \dfrac{\Pr\left[\mathsf{Avg}_c^a(D)=a_{\max}\right]}{\Pr\left[\mathsf{Avg}_c^a(D')=a_{\max}\right]} \le 1 < e^{\epsilon}$ because $a' \in [a_{\min}, a_{\max}]$.

Case 2: $\sigma_c(D') = \emptyset$. That is, $n = 0$ and D contains only one element satisfying c with value a. For any output value z, we have:

$$\Pr\left[\mathsf{Avg}_c^a(D) = z\right] = \begin{cases} \frac{1}{2}\exp\left(\frac{\epsilon(a_{\min}-a)}{\Delta_a}\right), & \text{when } z = a_{\min} \\ \frac{\epsilon}{2\Delta_a}\exp\left(\frac{-\epsilon|z-a|}{\Delta_a}\right), & \text{when } a_{\min} < z < a_{\max} \\ \frac{1}{2}\exp\left(\frac{-\epsilon(a_{\max}-a)}{\Delta_a}\right), & \text{when } z = a_{\max} \end{cases}$$

Now we compare the probability ratio. For any output z with $a_{\min} < z < a_{\max}$, noting that in such a case $\Pr\left[\mathsf{Avg}_c^a(D') = z\right] = h(z)$,

$$\frac{\Pr\left[\mathsf{Avg}_c^a(D) = z\right]}{\Pr\left[\mathsf{Avg}_c^a(D') = z\right]} = \frac{\frac{\epsilon}{2\Delta_a}\exp\left(\frac{-\epsilon|z-a|}{\Delta_a}\right)}{\frac{1}{\Delta_a}(1-\exp(-\epsilon/2))} = \frac{\frac{\epsilon}{2}\exp(-\epsilon(\frac{|z-a|}{\Delta_a}))}{1-\exp(-\epsilon/2)} \triangleq I.$$

Noting that $0 \leq |z-a| \leq \Delta_a$, we have

$$I \leq \frac{\frac{\epsilon}{2}}{1-\exp(-\epsilon/2)} \leq \exp(\epsilon) \text{ \bf and } I \geq \frac{\frac{\epsilon}{2}\exp(-\epsilon)}{1-\exp(-\epsilon/2)} \geq \exp(-\epsilon).$$

When $z = a_{\min}$,

$$\frac{\Pr\left[\mathsf{Avg}_c^a(D) = a_{\min}\right]}{\Pr\left[\mathsf{Avg}_c^a(D') = a_{\min}\right]} = \frac{\exp\left(\frac{\epsilon(a_{\min}-a)}{\Delta_a}\right)}{\exp(-\epsilon/2)} = \exp\left(\epsilon\left(\frac{a_{\min}-a}{\Delta_a}+\frac{1}{2}\right)\right)$$
$$\in [\exp(-\epsilon/2), \exp(\epsilon/2)] \qquad \text{since } -\Delta_a \leq a_{\min} - a \leq 0.$$

When $z = a_{\max}$,

$$\frac{\Pr\left[\mathsf{Avg}_c^a(D) = a_{\max}\right]}{\Pr\left[\mathsf{Avg}_c^a(D') = a_{\max}\right]} = \frac{\exp\left(\frac{-\epsilon(a_{\max}-a)}{\Delta_a}\right)}{\exp(-\epsilon/2)} = \exp\left(\epsilon\left(-\frac{a_{\max}-a}{\Delta_a}+\frac{1}{2}\right)\right)$$
$$\in [\exp(-\epsilon/2), \exp(\epsilon/2)] \qquad \text{since } 0 \leq a_{\max} - a \leq \Delta_a.$$

$\square$

2.5.5 NOISY AVERAGE WITH NORMALIZATION

Comparing Algorithm 2.3 with Algorithm 2.1, we note that it does not add any noise to the count, and can thus use the total privacy budget on noisy sum, instead of only half. We now show that this effect of halving the noise added for computing sum can be achieved by a simple normalization trick. Instead of summing up each x value, we assume that the default answer is $(a_{\min}, a_{\max})/2$, and only sums up $x - (a_{\min}, a_{\max})/2$ for each x in the input database. This reduces the sensitivity of the sum query from $\Delta_a = a_{\max} - a_{\min}$ to $\Delta_a/2$. This leads to Algorithm 2.4.

Algorithm 2.4 NoisyAverage with Normalization

Input: D: one dimensional dataset, ϵ: privacy parameter, $[a_{min}, a_{max}]$: data range

$\tilde{S} \leftarrow D.Sum() - D.Count() * (a_{min} + a_{max})/2 + \text{Lap}((a_{max} - a_{min})/\epsilon)$

$\tilde{C} \leftarrow D.Count() + \text{Lap}(2/\epsilon)$

if $\tilde{C} \leq 1$ **then**

    return $(a_{min}, a_{max})/2$

else

    return $\frac{\tilde{S}}{\tilde{C}} + (a_{min} + a_{max})/2$

end if

2.5.6   WHICH IS BEST

We have presented several algorithms for computing average. A natural question is which one is the best? Empirically we have found that Algorithms 2.3 performs better than Algorithm 2.4, which is followed by the method based on Exponential Mechanism, and finally by Algorithm 2.1. When ϵ is large, Algorithms 2.3 and Algorithm 2.4 are similar; and the $L1$ errors from them are about one half of those from the other two algorithms. When ϵ is small, the advantage of Algorithm 2.3 over Algorithm 2.4 is larger. However, an interesting and somewhat unexpected finding is that when ϵ is small, the algorithm for computing median in Example 2.21 is actually much better at computing the noisy average than all the other algorithms designed for computing them. When ϵ is small, the noise added to computing sum can dominate the difference between the median and average of the dataset.

2.6   SETTINGS TO APPLY DP

We classify DP mechanisms into the following four settings.

1. *Local Privacy.* In this setting, there is no trusted third party, and each participant perturbs and submits personal data. To apply DP here, one requires that for two arbitrary possible inputs x_1 and x_2, and any output y: $\Pr[y|x_1] \leq e^\epsilon \Pr[y|x_2]$.

2. *Interactive Query-answering.* For this and the remaining settings, there is a trusted data curator who has access to raw data. In the interactive setting, the data curator sits between the users and the database, and answers queries when they are submitted, without knowing what queries will be asked in the future.

3. *Single Workload.* In this setting, there is a single data analysis task one wants to perform on the dataset. Example tasks include learning a classifier, finding k cluster centroids of the data, and so on. The data curator performs the analysis task in a private way, and publishes the result.

4. *Noninteractive Publishing.* In this setting the curator publishes a synopsis of the input dataset, from which a broad class of queries can be answered and synthetic data can be generated.

Note that the latter three settings all require a trusted data curator.

Local Privacy. The local privacy setting is closely related to *randomized response* [Warner, 1965], which is a decades-old technique in social science to collect statistical information about embarrassing or illegal behavior. To report a single bit, one reports the true value with probability p and the flip of the true value with probability $1 - p$. In a sense, applying the DP requirement here can be viewed as a generalization of the property from randomized response to a case where one reports a non-binary value.

The Interactive Setting. In this setting, the data curator does not know ahead of time what queries will be encountered, and answers queries as they come. One simple method is to divide up the privacy budget and consume a portion of the privacy budget to answer each query [Blum et al., 2005]. More sophisticated methods (e.g., Hardt and Rothblum [2010], Hardt and Talwar [2010], Roth and Roughgarden [2010]) maintain a history of past queries and answers, and try to use the history to answer new queries whenever the error of doing so is acceptable.

Using the interactive setting in practice, however, has several challenges. First and foremost, answering each query consumes a portion of privacy budget, and after the privacy budget is exhausted, no additional queries can be answered on the data without violating DP. Second, the interactive setting is unsuitable with more than one data users. When a dataset needs to serve the general public, such as when the census bureau provides the census data to the public, the number of data users is very large. Because the curator cannot be sure whether any two data users are colluding or not, the privacy budget has to be shared by *all users*. This means that only a few users can be supported and each user can have only a small number of queries answered.

Single Workload. In this setting, the goal is to publish the result from one data mining or machine learning task. Most approaches try to adapt an existing machine learning algorithm by making each step private. An alternative approach includes perturbing the optimization objective function for learning a classifier. This is studied in Chapter 5.

Non-interactive publishing. In this setting, the data curator publishes some summary of the data. It is generally assumed that the set of queries one cares about is known. The most natural set of queries are histogram queries or marginal queries. This is studied in Chapters 4 and 6.

Interactive vs. Non-interactive. There are a series of negative results concerning differential privacy in the non-interactive mode [Dinur and Nissim, 2003, Dwork and Yekhanin, 2008, Dwork et al., 2009, 2006, 2007], and these results have been interpreted "to mean that one cannot answer a linear, in the database size, number of queries with small noise while preserving privacy" and motivate "an interactive approach to private data analysis where the number of queries is limited to be small—sub-linear in the size n of the dataset" [Dwork et al., 2009]. However, these results are all based on query sets that are broader than the natural set of queries that one is interested in. For example, suppose the dataset is one-dimensional where each value is an integer number in $[1 \ldots M]$. Further suppose that the data is sufficiently dense, then publishing a histogram likely gives information that one wants to know about the database. These negative results say that if one also considers subset sum queries (i.e., the sum of an arbitrary set of indices in $[1 \ldots m]$), then not all queries can be answered to a high accuracy. Intuitively this is true; however, it does not say much about how accurately we can answer range queries.

2.7   BIBLIOGRAPHICAL NOTES

The DP notion first appeared in Dwork [2006], Dwork et al. [2006], although it has its roots in earlier work [Dinur and Nissim, 2003, Dwork and Nissim, 2004]. The Laplace mechanism was introduced in Dwork et al. [2006]. The exponential mechanism was introduced in McSherry and Talwar [2007]. The composition properties were stated in the paper introducing the PINQ system [McSherry, 2009], although it was generally known.

CHAPTER 3

What Does DP Mean?

3.1 LIMITATIONS OF SYNTACTIC NOTIONS

To understand why DP is appealing, it is also helpful to examine the alternatives. Before DP was introduced, researchers had been focusing on syntactic privacy notions. The most prominent of which is k-anonymity [Samarati, 2001, Sweeney, 2002]. When applied to relational data, this notion requires the division of all attributes into *quasi-identifiers* and *sensitive attributes*, where the adversary is assumed to know the former, but not the latter.

Definition 3.1 k-Anonymity. A table satisfies k-anonymity relative to a set of quasi-identifier attributes if and only if when the table is projected to include only the quasi-identifier attributes, every record in the projected table appears at least k times.

The initial objective of k-anonymity was to prevent *re-identification*, i.e., an adversary who knows the quasi-identifier values of an individual should not be able to point to a record in the output and say "this is the record of the individual I know." In a dataset that satisfies k-anonymity, if there is any record matching an individual, there are at least k such records, making re-identification difficult. Researchers have observed that k-anonymity does not prevent *attribute disclosure*, i.e., information about sensitive attributes can still be learned, perhaps due to the uneven distribution of their values. This leads to privacy notions such as ℓ-diversity [Machanavajjhala et al., 2006], t-closeness [Li et al., 2007], and so on. All these notions, however, are syntactic, in the sense that they define a property about the final "anonymized" dataset, and do not consider the algorithm or mechanism via which the output is obtained. In contrast, DP is a property of the algorithm, instead of the output.

Any anonymization algorithm must be designed to optimize for some utility objective. Without considering utility, one can trivially achieve privacy protection by publishing nothing. Knowing that an algorithm would optimize for a certain utility objective enables one to infer additional information about the input when given the output, as shown, e.g., in the minimality attack [Cormode et al., 2010, Wong et al., 2007].

Another illustration of the limitation of the syntactic nature of k-anonymity is given in Li et al. [2012a], which points out that one trivial way to satisfy k-anonymity is to simply duplicate each record k times, or similarly, to select a subset of the records and duplicate them. Furthermore, even though k-anonymity can be satisfied without providing real privacy protection, some k-anonymization algorithms can provide protection similar to ϵ-DP [Li et al., 2012a]. However, here the privacy protection property is clearly associated with the algorithm, and not with just the output.

3.2   SEMANTIC GUARANTEES OF DIFFERENTIAL PRIVACY

To assess whether DP offers sufficient protection of privacy, we have to examine social and legal conceptions of privacy. Privacy as a social and legal concept is multi-faceted. Solove [2010] identified six conceptions of privacy: (1) the right to be let alone [Warren and Brandeis, 1890]; (2) limited access to the self; (3) secrecy—the concealment of certain matters from others; (4) control over personal information; (5) personhood—the protection of one's personality, individuality, and dignity; (6) intimacy—control over, or limited access to, one's intimate relationships or aspects of life. These conceptions overlap with each other; and some are not applicable in the context of data privacy.

Among these, we distill two related, yet different, conceptions that are most relevant to data privacy: "**privacy as secrecy**" and "**privacy as control** (over personal information)." The former was stated as the "right to conceal discreditable facts about himself" [Posner, 1998], and the latter was stated by Westin [1967] as: "Privacy is the claim of individuals, groups, or institutions to determine for themselves when, how and to what extent information about them is communicated to others." These two conceptions can be linked to two different approaches of defining privacy mathematically, which we explore in this section. The former leads to a "prior-to-posterior" approach, and the latter leads to a "posterior-to-posterior" approach.

3.2.1   INFEASIBILITY OF ACHIEVING "PRIVACY AS SECRECY"

To formalize privacy-as-secrecy mathematically, one naturally takes a Bayesian approach. That is, one first specifies what the adversary believes *a priori*. After observing the output of $A(D)$, the adversary can update his belief using Bayes' rule. Privacy-as-secrecy leads to defining privacy as bounding an arbitrary adversary's **prior-to-posterior belief change** regarding any specific individual. This view is taken in Dalenius [1977], which defines privacy as: *Access to a statistical database should not enable one to learn anything about an individual that could not be learned without access.* Unfortunately, achieving this notion is only possible by destroying the utility. Consider the following example.

Example 3.2   (Adapted from Dwork and Roth [2013].) Assume that smoking causes lung cancer is not yet public knowledge, and an organization conducted a study that demonstrates this connection. A smoker Carl was not involved in the study, but complains that publishing the result of this study affects his privacy, because others would know that he has a higher chance of getting lung cancer, and as a result he may suffer damages, e.g., his health insurance premium may increase.

Clearly, access to the study data enables one to change one's belief about Carl's chance of getting cancer. Furthermore, even if one publishes the study result in a way that satisfies ϵ-DP, the degree of change from the prior belief to the posterior belief is independent from the ϵ value, and depends mostly on the strength of the correlation. Trying to avoid this inference regarding Carl would destroy the utility of publishing the data in the first place.

The impossibility to bound an arbitrary adversary's prior-to-posterior belief change while providing utility has been proven in several forms [Dwork, 2006, Dwork and Naor, 2008, Kifer and Machanavajjhala, 2011, Li et al., 2013]. In Dwork [2006], Dwork and Naor [2008], this result is stated as *"absolute disclosure prevention (while preserving utility at the same time) is impossible because of the arbitrary auxiliary information the adversary may have."* In Kifer and Machanavajjhala [2011], this result takes the form of a "no free lunch theorem," which states that achieving both utility and privacy is impossible without *making assumptions about the data.* In Li et al. [2013], the result is *"without restricting the adversary's prior belief about the dataset distribution, achieving privacy requires publishing essentially the same information for two arbitrary datasets."*

3.2.2   TOWARD A "REAL-WORLD-IDEAL-WORLD" APPROACH

The privacy-as-secrecy notion is very similar to the notion of semantic security for cryptosystems [Goldwasser and Micali, 1984]. While this appealing notion is achievable for encryption, it is not achievable for data privacy. The reason is as follows. In encryption, there are two classes of recipients: those who have the decryption key, and those who do not. The utility requirement is that the plaintext can be recovered, and applies only to those who have the key. The secrecy requirement is that nothing regarding the plaintext can be learned, and applies only to those without the key. In the data privacy context, however, there is only one class of recipients for which both secrecy and utility requirements apply.

A closer analogy can be found in the context of order-preserving encryption (OPE) [Boldyreva et al., 2009], where recipients without the decryption key should be able to distinguish orderings between the plaintexts; however, other information regarding plaintexts should remain hidden. In Boldyreva et al. [2009], security of OPE requires that what an adversary can observe when an OPE scheme is used (called the real-world view) is indistinguishable from what the adversary can observe when an idealized scheme is used that reveals only ordering information and nothing else (called the ideal-world view).

This real-world-ideal-world approach has been used in defining security of secure multi-party computation (SMC) protocols. In SMC, similarly one cannot require that no information about input is leaked, because information about input may be inferred from the output. Instead, one requires the real-world view to be cryptographically indistinguishable from the ideal-world view, in which computation is carried out by a trusted third party, who provides only the output and nothing else.

3.2.3 DP AS APPROXIMATING THE IDEAL WORLD OF "PRIVACY AS CONTROL"

DP applies this "real-world-ideal-world" approach to data privacy. The key is to define what are the "ideal worlds" for privacy. One natural choice is to accept the "privacy as control" conception, and define the ideal worlds to be the ones where "control over personal data" is exercised. Interestingly, instead of having one ideal world (as typical in SMC), we have many ideal worlds, one for each individual, in which the individual's data is removed (or rewritten with some arbitrary value). DP can be interpreted as requiring *the real world view to be close to the view in each and every ideal world*.

Ganta et al. [2008], Kasiviswanathan and Smith [2008, 2014] provided what may be the first attempt at formalizing the following characterization as DP's guarantee: *Regardless of external knowledge, an adversary with access to the sanitized database draws the same conclusions whether or not my data is included in the original database.* This can be viewed as defining multiple ideal worlds; in each of which one individual's data is removed, as if the individual has opted out.

More specifically, databases are assumed to be vectors in $\mathcal{D}^n$, where $\mathcal{D}$ is the domain or universe from which each tuple is drawn, and n is the length of the input dataset. That is, this uses the Bounded DP setting where the size of the dataset is public information. *A-priori* knowledge is captured via a prior probability distribution b on $\mathcal{D}^n$. The posterior belief of the adversary after observing a transcript of interacting with a mechanism $\mathcal{A}$ is thus computed by

$$\bar{b}[\mathsf{x}|t] = \frac{\Pr\left[\mathcal{A}(\mathsf{x}) = t\right] b(\mathsf{x})}{\sum_{z \in \mathcal{D}^n} \Pr\left[\mathcal{A}(\mathsf{z}) = t\right] b(\mathsf{z})}. \tag{3.1}$$

There are then n different ideal worlds; in each of which one tuple in the input dataset is replaced with a special value $\perp$. Using x_{-i} to denote the result of replacing the i-th component of the vector x with $\perp$, the posterior belief for the adversary in the i-th ideal world is defined to be the following:

$$\bar{b}_i[\mathsf{x}|t] = \frac{\Pr\left[\mathcal{A}(\mathsf{x}_{-i}) = t\right] b(\mathsf{x})}{\sum_{z \in \mathcal{D}^n} \Pr\left[\mathcal{A}(\mathsf{z}_{-i}) = t\right] b(\mathsf{z})}. \tag{3.2}$$

In Ganta et al. [2008], Kasiviswanathan and Smith [2008, 2014], a mechanism is said to have $\bar{\epsilon}$-**semantic privacy** if for any belief b, any possible transcript t of $\mathcal{A}$, and any $i = 1, \ldots, n$, we have $\mathbf{SD}(\bar{b}[\cdot|t], \bar{b}_i[\cdot|t]) \leq \bar{\epsilon}$, where $\mathbf{SD}$ gives the statistical distance (i.e., total variation distance) between two distributions; that is $\mathbf{SD}(P, Q) = \max_{T \subseteq \mathcal{T}} |P(T) - Q(T)|$, where $\mathcal{T}$ is the set of all possible transcripts.

The main results regarding ϵ-DP in Ganta et al. [2008], Kasiviswanathan and Smith [2008, 2014] are as follows: (1) Any $\mathcal{A}$ that satisfies ϵ-DP also satisfies $\bar{\epsilon}$-semantic privacy for $\bar{\epsilon} = e^{\epsilon} - 1$. (2) For $0 < \epsilon \leq 0.45$, $\epsilon/2$-semantic privacy implies 3ϵ-differential privacy.

While we agree with the general conclusion that DP bounds the difference in posteriors between real and ideal worlds, we find the above formulation not completely satisfactory for the following reasons. First and foremost, while the paper does not explicitly state what exactly the prior belief b intends to model, the fact that it is a distribution over $\mathcal{D}^n$ (the set of all possible input databases) and the way it is used in Eqs. (3.1) and (3.2) mean that it models the adversary's prior knowledge about what the input dataset might be. This, however, captures only the adversary's prior knowledge about the input dataset, but not any other knowledge about the world in general, including information of individuals the adversary believes to be not in the dataset. For example, the following external knowledge: "*Terry is not in the dataset, and Terry is two inches shorter than the average Lithuanian woman.*" includes information about individuals who are believed to be not in the dataset. This information cannot be encoded by assigning probabilities to possible input datasets.

Second, the relationship between the parameters of ϵ-DP and $\bar{\epsilon}$-semantic privacy seems a bit messy. For example, the guarantee that ϵ-DP implies $(e^\epsilon - 1)$-semantic privacy provides no guarantee when $\epsilon \geq \ln 2$, as the maximal possible value for statistical distance is 1. Thus one obtains no support from this when using $\epsilon = 1$, which is common in the literature. Also, for $\bar{\epsilon} > 0.225$, it is unclear whether $\bar{\epsilon}$-semantic privacy implies ϵ-DP for any ϵ.

3.2.4   A FORMULATION OF DP'S SEMANTIC GUARANTEE

We provide such a semantic formulation of privacy as follows. We model an adversary as a decision function that takes a transcript $\mathcal{A}(D) = t$ as input, and outputs a decision from a set of possible decisions. We assume that each dataset D consists of data of individuals, and use D_{-v} to denote the result of removing v's data from D. We then define the neighboring relation such that for any dataset D, and any individual v, D and D_{-v} are neighboring. For any algorithm $\mathcal{A}$ that satisfies ϵ-DP, it follows from Property 2.2 (transformation invariance) that for any adversary (i.e., decision function), any dataset D, any individual v, and any decision c, the probability that the adversary decides c in the real world (where $\mathcal{A}(D)$ is observed) is e^ϵ-close to the probability that the adversary decides c in the ideal world (where $A(D_{-v})$ is observed). Here two probability values p and p' are λ-close (for $\lambda \geq 1$) when

$$p \leq \lambda p' \bigwedge p' \leq \lambda p \bigwedge (1 - p) \leq \lambda(1 - p') \bigwedge (1 - p') \leq \lambda(1 - p). \qquad (3.3)$$

That is, ϵ-DP ensures that for *any arbitrary adversary*, her **posterior-to-posterior belief difference** is bounded by e^ϵ.

3.2.5   THE PERSONAL DATA PRINCIPLE

The main insight underlying DP is that one can treat a hypothetical world in which one individual's data is removed as an ideal world where that individual's privacy is protected perfectly. By doing this, we can ignore any correlation between this individual's data and other data in the dataset. We observe that this insight can be supported by adopting the "privacy as control" interpretation. We formulate the following principle as the bedrock for DP.

[The Personal Data Principle (PDP)] Data privacy means giving an individual control over his or her personal data. An individual's privacy is not violated if no per-

sonal data about the individual is used. Privacy does not mean that no information about the individual is learned, or no harm is done to an individual; enforcing the latter is infeasible and unreasonable.

We note that the widely accepted OECD (Organization for Economic Co-operation and Development) privacy principles (e.g., collection limitation, data quality, purpose specification, use limitation, individual participation, and so on) all refer to **personal data**.

As another support for PDP, we also note that a common way to protect privacy is "opting out." It is commonly accepted that once an individual has "opted out," i.e., the individual's data has been removed, that individual's privacy is protected.

Applying PDP to the smoking-causes-cancer example (Example 3.2), we would say that Carl's complaint about his privacy being affected by the publishing of this dataset is invalid, because what is at stake *is not control of his personal data*.

3.2.6   A CASE STUDY IN APPLYING PDP

We now apply the PDP principle to analyze a debate regarding DP. Kifer and Machanavajjhala [2011] asserted that: "*Additional popularized claims have been made about the privacy guarantees of differential privacy. These include: (1) It makes no assumptions about how data are generated. (2) It protects an individual's information (even) if an attacker knows about all other individuals in the data. (3) It is robust to arbitrary background knowledge.*" They went on to refute these claims, by pointing out when there is correlation in the data, the level of privacy protection provided when satisfying ϵ-DP may not be e^ϵ.

Example 3.3   (Adapted from Kifer and Machanavajjhala [2011].) Bob and his family members may have contracted a highly contagious disease, in which case the entire family would have been infected. An attacker can ask the query "how many people at Bob's address have this disease?" When receiving an answer computed while satisfying ϵ-DP, the attacker's probability estimate (of Bob being sick) can change by a factor of $e^{k\epsilon}$ because of data correlation, where k is the number of members in Bob's family including Bob.

A natural question is whether satisfying ϵ-DP provides a level of privacy protection promised by the ϵ value. It is true that an adversary's belief about whether Bob has the disease may change by a factor of $e^{k\epsilon}$. This is an example that DP cannot bound prior-to-posterior belief change against arbitrary external knowledge, which we know is impossible to achieve. However, DP's guarantee that real-world-posterior and ideal-world-posterior are e^ϵ-close remains valid, and one can apply PDP to say that ϵ-DP indeed provides a level of privacy protection promised by the ϵ value. We will discuss challenges to this reasoning in Section 3.3.3.

We want to point out that the three claims regarding DP listed in Kifer and Machanavajjhala [2011] have roots in claims made regarding DP's ability to provide prior-to-posterior bound. In the Appendix of the seminal paper on differential privacy [Dwork et al., 2006], the authors introduce the following semantic privacy notion: *A mechanism is said to be (k,ϵ)-**simulatable** if for* *every informed adversary who already knows all except for k entries in the dataset D, every output, and every predicate f over the set of all input datasets, the change in the adversary's belief on f is multiplicative-bounded by* e^ϵ. To simplify our discussion, we focus on the case where $k = 1$. Let n denote the number of records in the dataset. Being $(1, \epsilon)$-semantically secure means that no matter what the adversary's prior belief is (*so long as it is consistent with the belief of n − 1 entries*), after observing the output, the adversary's belief change is bounded. An algorithm satisfies ϵ-DP iff. it is $(1, \epsilon)$-simulatable.

We note that $(1, \epsilon)$-simulatable, which is equivalent to ϵ-DP, bounds prior-to-posterior belief change. The reasoning in Dwork et al. [2006], while technically correct, is potentially misleading, because it gives the *impression* that DP provides prior-to-posterior bound for an arbitrary prior belief of the adversary via the following arguments: Since DP is able to provide such a bound against so strong an adversary as an "informed adversary," intuitively it should be able to provide the same bound against any other adversary, which must be weaker. We know that providing such a prior-to-posterior bound is impossible without destroying utility. The key in the apparent contradiction lies in the choice of how to define an "informed adversary," which might appear to be a strong model for adversaries, but is in fact, quite limiting. It limits the adversary to being certain about $n − 1$ records and requiring the adversary's belief to be consistent with that. A perfectly reasonable adversary who believes that either Bob's family all have the disease or none has the disease cannot be modeled as an "informed adversary."

3.3   EXAMINING DP AND PDP

DP overcomes the challenges of data correlation by applying the PDP. However, there are several caveats that undermine the application of PDP to justify DP in particular usage scenarios.

3.3.1   WHEN THE NOTION OF NEIGHBORING DATASETS IS DEFINED INCORRECTLY

When the notion of neighboring datasets is defined incorrectly, one cannot use PDP to claim that the real world approximates worlds where privacy is protected. Examples of such problematic usages of DP are abundant in the literature.

In the context of graph data, two variants of DP are introduced: in edge-DP, two graphs are neighboring if they differ on one edge; in node-DP, two graphs are neighboring if by removing one node and all edges connected to it in one graph, one obtains the other graph. Satisfying node-DP is much harder than satisfying edge-DP, since removing one node may cause the removal of many edges. Because of this, most papers studying DP on graph data consider edge-DP, under the justification that doing so protects the individual relationship between two entities. We believe that using edge-DP is incorrect when each node represents an individual, as removing an edge is not equivalent to exercising control of personal data, and the graph resulted from removing an edge cannot be considered an ideal world. In fact, attacks on anonymized graph data are in the form of re-identifying nodes, illustrating that this is where the privacy concern lies. Finally, even if one accepts the claim that the goal is to protect the relationship between two entities, edge-DP falls short of achieving that because edges are correlated with each other, and the Personal Data Principle cannot be used to justify the decision to ignore such correlation.

Data, such as Netflix movie ratings, can be represented via a matrix, where each cell represents the rating of one user on a movie. Similar to graph data, one can consider cell-DP and row-DP [McSherry and Mironov, 2009]. The criticisms of using edge-DP for graph data similarly apply to cell-DP.

In McSherry and Mahajan [2010], DP techniques are applied to network trace analysis where neighboring datasets differ in a single record representing a single packet for two datasets considered in McSherry and Mahajan [2010]. While it is acknowledged that this is only a starting point for beginning to understand the applicability of DP to network data, we caution that this does not provides meaningful privacy protection, since protecting the information about a single packet is unlikely to be the real privacy concern, and data correlation destroys the quality of protection even for information about a single packet.

Theoretically one can compensate for the effect by analyzing and bounding the effect of correlation and choosing a smaller ϵ. However, doing so means giving up the main insight underlying DP: by identifying ideal worlds, one can ignore correlations, and requires new definitions and techniques beyond DP to explicitly analyze and deal with correlations.

3.3.2   WHEN USING DP IN THE LOCAL SETTING

The most high-profile applications of DP are in the *local setting*, where there is no trusted data curator, and each participant perturbs and submits personal data. The only deployed system using DP that we are aware of is Google's RAPPOR (Randomized Aggregatable Privacy-Preserving Ordinal Response) system [Erlingsson et al., 2014], which collects information from individuals in the local setting. This is a generalization of *randomized response* [Warner, 1965], which is a decades-old technique in social science to collect statistical information about embarrassing or illegal behavior. To report a single bit, one reports the true value with probability p and the flip of the true value with probability $1 - p$. Analogous to DP, one can define a requirement that for two arbitrary possible inputs x_1 and x_2, and any output y: $\Pr[y|x_1] \leq e^\epsilon \Pr[y|x_2]$.

The key issue here is how many questions for which answers will be collected via the system, and how to choose the parameter ϵ. Systems such as RAPPOR are designed to answer many hundreds of questions (or more) while using the same fixed privacy budget $\epsilon = \ln 9$ for each question. When answers to these questions are correlated, it is unclear what kind of protection is achieved. Correlation has the potential to enable more accurate answers to be obtained. Attempts to use PDP to say this is not a concern amount to taking the absurd position that revealing answers to all except one question is an ideal world for the individual.

Similar concerns exist when applying DP to stream data in the local setting. When neighboring datasets are defined as differing on a single event, correlation between different events must be explicitly considered, and cannot be ignored by applying PDP. In other words, using DP in the local setting is closer to the "privacy-as-secrecy" interpretation, since one's goal is to hide one piece of info. When one's ultimate goal is to hide pieces of information, then one needs to consider the effect of data correlation.

3.3.3   WHAT CONSTITUTES ONE INDIVIDUAL'S DATA

To apply PDP, we first need to identify what is **one individual's personal data**. Doing so becomes difficult when dealing with genomic and health data. Genomic information is highly correlated. For example, DeCode Genetics, a company based in Reykjavík, Iceland, collected full DNA sequences from 10,000 consenting Iceland residents. Combining this with genealogy records, DeCode is able to guess BRAC2 gene mutations (which dramatically increases the chance of ovarian and breast cancer among women) for approximately 2,000 individuals who did not participate in original DNA collection. They face a moral and legal dilemma of whether to notify these individuals, as there is preventive surgery which can significantly decrease the chances of mortality.

Given correlation in genomic data, should my parents' genomic data also be considered to be part of my genomic data? What about my children, siblings, grandparents, and other relatives? What about non-genomic medical information regarding hereditary disease? These legal and ethical questions still need to be resolved, although evidence suggests that such privacy concerns will be recognized. In 2003, the supreme court of Iceland ruled that a daughter has the right to prohibit the transfer of her deceased father's health information to a Health Sector Database, not because of her right to act as a substitute of her deceased father, but in the recognition that she might, on the basis of her right to protection of privacy, have an interest in preventing the transfer of health data concerning her father into the database, as information could be inferred from such data relating to the hereditary characteristics of her father which might also apply to herself.[1] When dealing with genomic and health data, one cannot simply say correlation doesn't matter because of PDP, and may have to quantify and deal with such correlation.

3.3.4   AN INDIVIDUAL'S PERSONAL DATA OR PERSONAL DATA UNDER ONE INDIVIDUAL'S CONTROL

Sometimes, one individual is given legal control over other individual's personal data, e.g., a parent is the legal guardian over minors. Applying DP may be problematic when this occurs. Let us return to Example 3.3, and assume that the dataset contains the information of Bob and his $k - 1$ minor children for whom Bob is the legal guardian. Can we still claim that satisfying ϵ-DP offers privacy protection at ϵ-level by wielding the PDP? We believe that this position can be challenged. Even though the children's data are not Bob's personal data, they are under the control of Bob. Applying the "opting-out" analysis, when Bob wants to opt out because of privacy concern, he can and likely will remove data of all his children as well. In other words, Bob may not accept that removing only his record results in an "ideal" world for him. However, we acknowledge that reasonable people can disagree on this, based on different legal and philosophical arguments.

---

[1]https://epic.org/privacy/genetic/iceland_decision.pdf

3.3.5   GROUP PRIVACY AS A POTENTIAL LEGAL ACHILLES' HEEL FOR DP

Let us return to Example 3.3, and change the setting to: Bob lives in a dorm building with $k-1$ other unrelated individuals. Clearly we can wield PDP and argue that DP provides appropriate protection. This position is perfectly justifiable if individuals other than Bob **have agreed** to have their data used. However, it is likely that nobody in Bob's dorm has explicitly given consent to the data usage (if they do, then DP is not needed). Now, accurate information regarding whether individuals in the dorm have the disease or not can be learned; and this information may cause damage for these individuals. When this happens, can the individuals in Bob's dorm come together and complain that their **collective privacy** or **group privacy** is violated?

Indeed legal and philosophical literature has acknowledged that a group can hold the right to privacy and it is known as "*group privacy*." Bloustein [2002] defines group privacy as: "*Group privacy is an extension of individual privacy. The interest protected by group privacy is the desire and need of people to come together, to exchange information, share feelings, make plans and act in concert to attain their objectives.*" This concept of group privacy, however, appears to be somewhat different from what we are considering. To our knowledge, currently there are no explicit regulations protecting the privacy of a group of people in the context of data publishing or sharing. In the era of big data and data publishing, and especially with the application of DP, the issue of group privacy is likely to become a pressing concern that needs to be addressed by legal, philosophy, and other social science scholars. If such "collective privacy" or "group privacy" is recognized, then using DP for personal data appears fundamentally flawed.

3.3.6   A MORAL CHALLENGE TO PRIVATE PARTY BENEFITING FROM DP

Even when using DP in a setting where the above challenges do not apply, there is a moral challenge to private parties benefitting from the application of DP. One natural application of DP is when a company wants to sell (or otherwise profit from) data collected from individuals in a way that the individuals do not authorize. That is, DP is useful in situations similar to when the Group Insurance Commission (GIC) sells (supposedly) anonymous medical history data [Sweeney, 2002], or when AOL publishes search logs [Barbaro and Tom Zeller, 2006]. Suppose that a company processes the data in a way that satisfies ϵ-DP for $\epsilon = 0.01$ and then makes money from it. Is this acceptable? Many applications of DP seem to suggest that the answer is "yes."

Now let us consider the following hypothetical situation: A company takes 2 cents from every bank account, and justifies the action by saying that every individual is minimally affected.[2] Is this acceptable? We believe that almost everyone will say "no," because stealing is stealing, no matter how small the amount is. A similar argument would apply if a company benefits from data

---

[2]This is inspired by a question on Quora: https://www.quora.com/Say-I-steal-2-cents-from-every-bank-account-in-America-I-am-proven-guilty-but-everyone-I-stole-from-says-theyre-fine-with-it-What-happens.

processed in a way that satisfies DP. We note that one can still support using DP where the public in general benefits from the data sharing. When only private parties benefit from such sharing, than a moral challenge can be levered against the party.

3.4 ADDITIONAL CAVEATS WHEN USING DP

Beyond the validity of using PDP to justify DP, there are a few additional caveats when applying DP, which we now discuss.

3.4.1 USING AN ϵ THAT IS TOO LARGE

One caveat when applying ϵ-DP is to use a large ϵ value. How large is too large? The inventors of DP stated [Dwork and Smith, 2010]: *"The choice of ϵ is essentially a social question. We tend to think of ϵ as, say,* 0.01, 0.1, *or in some cases,* ln 2 *or* ln 3." These values are also broadly consistent with most papers in this domain [Hsu et al., 2014]. We now offer some support for these numbers. Table 3.1 gives the range of p' that is e^ϵ close to p. For example, when $\epsilon = 0.1$, the adversary's belief may increase from 0.001–0.0011, or from 0.5–0.5476. Our, necessarily subjective, interpretation of these numbers is that $\epsilon = 0.1$ offers reasonably strong privacy protection and should suffice for most cases, and $\epsilon = 1$ may be acceptable in a lot of cases. Using $\epsilon = 5$ is probably unsuitable in most cases. Finally, $\epsilon \geq 10$ offers virtually no privacy protection and should not be used. If acceptable utility can be obtained only when $\epsilon \geq 10$, we think that demonstrates a failure of effectively applying DP in that setting.

Table 3.1: The range of the probability p' that is e^ϵ-close to the probability value p

ϵ	0.01	0.1	1	5	10
$\lambda = e^\epsilon$	1.01	1.11	2.72	148	22026
$p = 0.001$	(0.0010, 0.0010)	(0.0009, 0.0011)	(0.0004, 0.0027)	(0.0000, 0.1484)	(0.0000, 1.0000)
$p = 0.01$	(0.0099, 0.0101)	(0.0090, 0.0111)	(0.0037, 0.0272)	(0.0001, 0.9933)	(0.0000, 1.0000)
$p = 0.1$	(0.0990, 0.1010)	(0.0905, 0.1105)	(0.0368, 0.2718)	(0.0007, 0.9939)	(0.0000, 1.0000)
$p = 0.5$	(0.4950, 0.5050)	(0.4524, 0.5476)	(0.1839, 0.8161)	(0.0034, 0.9966)	(0.0000, 1.0000)
$p = 0.75$	(0.7475, 0.7525)	(0.7237, 0.7738)	(0.3204, 0.9080)	(0.0051, 0.9983)	(0.0000, 1.0000)
$p = 0.99$	(0.9899, 0.9901)	(0.9889, 0.9910)	(0.9728, 0.9963)	(0.0067, 0.9999)	(0.0000, 1.0000)

3.4.2 APPLYING A MODEL TO PERSONAL DATA

The fact that a model is learned while satisfying DP does not remove privacy concern caused by applying the model to personal data. A typical data-drive prediction scenario involves two steps. In the first step, one learns some model/knowledge from the data of a group of individuals (we call this group A). DP can be used in this step. In the second step, one applies the model to make predictions regarding each individual in a group B. DP cannot be applied in this step. To make a prediction regarding an individual, one has to use some of the individual's attributes. Satisfying DP would destroy any possible utility in this step. This step creates new privacy concerns that should not be confused with those during the learning of a model.

This problem can be confusing when *A* and *B* are the same group, in which case an individual's personal information is used twice, first in learning the model and again in making predictions about the individual. Satisfying DP in the former does not address privacy concerns in the latter. In Duhigg [2012], it is reported that a father learned the pregnancy of his daughter, who was in high school, through coupons for baby clothes and cribs mailed by Target. This is predicted by applying a model to the family's purchase record. As Target's frequent shopper program (and likely any other such program) consents to the merchant using the data for marketing purposes, this cannot be considered a privacy violation in the legal sense. However, if such user consent does not exist, then even if the model is learned while satisfying DP, this should be considered a privacy violation because of usage of shopping records in the prediction.

3.4.3   PRIVACY AND DISCRIMINATION

Supposed one has learned a classifier in a way that satisfies DP. What if one applies the classifier to the public attributes of an individual (such as gender, age, race, nationality, etc.), and makes decisions accordingly? Even if one argues that the privacy concern is addressed by DP, doing so can be considered a form of discrimination.

A subtle and interesting point is that sometimes better privacy can result in more discrimination. Wheelan [2010] had an interesting discussion: "*Statistical discrimination, or so-called 'rational discrimination,' takes place when an individual makes an inference that is defensible based on broad statistical patterns but (1) is likely to be wrong in the specific case at hand; and (2) has a discriminatory effect on some group. Suppose an employer has no racial prejudice but does have an aversion to hiring workers with a criminal background. [...] If this employer has to make a hiring decision without access to applicants' criminal backgrounds [...], then it is entirely plausible that he will discriminate against black male applicants who are far more likely to have served in prison. [...] If this employer can acquire that information with certainty, then the broader patterns don't matter. Data shows that access to criminal background checks reduce discrimination against black men without criminal records.*"

In summary, applying statistical knowledge could lead to discrimination that is considered illegal by law. This is an issue orthogonal to privacy. On the one hand, one should not criticize DP because discrimination remains possible with DP. On the other hand, one should be aware that the discrimination concern is not addressed by using DP.

3.5   BIBLIOGRAPHICAL NOTES

Li et al. [2012a] discussed limitations of *k*-anonymity and relationship between *k*-anonymization and DP. Dwork [2006] and Dwork and Naor [2008] discussed the impossibility of preventing any inference of personal information. Ganta et al. [2008], Kasiviswanathan and Smith [2008, 2014] provided an attempt at formalizing a Bayesian guarantee of DP. Kifer and Machanavajjhala [2011] examined the impact of correlation on guarantee of DP. Li et al. [2013] examined DP from the perspective of protecting against membership disclosure, i.e., the information whether an individual's data is in the dataset or not.

CHAPTER 4

Publishing Histograms for Low-dimensional Datasets

Many methods for publishing datasets while satisfying DP use some form of histogram publishing at its core. Strictly speaking, a histogram is a graphical representation of the distribution of numerical data. To construct a histogram, one first creates bins by dividing the entire range of values into a series of intervals, and then counts how many values fall into each interval. In this book we use the term "histogram" in a more general sense. For us, a histogram includes two things: (1) a partitioning of the data domain into multiple non-overlapping bins, and (2) the number of data points in each bin. Histograms give a rough sense of the density of the underlying distribution of the data. Publishing histograms is particularly attractive in the context of DP because doing so has a low sensitivity of 1.

4.1 PROBLEM DEFINITION

In this chapter we focus mostly on low-dimensional datasets, e.g, datasets with one or two attributes.

4.1.1 THREE SETTINGS

We consider the following two different kinds of datasets.

1. **With Suitable Partitioning.** In this setting, we are given a pre-defined partitioning, and the average number of data points in a bin is sufficiently high, so that the true accounts are not dominated by Laplacian noises. In this setting, a basic method is to simply apply the Laplace mechanism. However, when the number of bins is large, one may benefit from the techniques of **Hierarchical Histograms and Constrained Inferencing**.

2. **Without Suitable Partitioning.** This setting needs additional techniques. Either there exists a pre-defined partitioning, but the average number of data points for each bin is low. Or the number of natural unit bins is so large that it is infeasible to enumerate through all of them. For example, this will be the case when the data values are real numbers. Here the main challenge is to determine the partitioning to accommodate for the input data distribution.

4.1.2   MEASURING UTILITY

Intuitively, the utility objective for publishing histograms is to be able to accurately answer range queries in the form of how many data points there are in a range using the summary. However, formalizing such an objective is quite nontrivial. There are three sources of non-determinism.

- **Dataset distribution.** Should one care about an algorithm's worst-case performance on pathological datasets or its performance on typical datasets? For practical applications, one probably cares about the latter. However, it is difficult to define what is a typical dataset. If one has a probability distribution over what the dataset is likely to be, then average-case performance over the likely datasets is probably the most meaningful metric. However, obtaining such a distribution over the input datasets requires making assumptions that are difficult, if not impossible, to justify. Most papers use experimental evaluations, in which one has to select the datasets, and the differences in performances could be due to the nature of the datasets and may not hold on other datasets.

- **Query distribution.** The first question here is "what are the set of queries one is interested in?" For publishing histograms, one natural choice is the set of all range queries, although some approaches assume that one is interested in a specific subset of such queries. A follow-up question is "should one care about the average performance (which requires as input a probability distribution of the queries) or the worst-case performance?" We note that when one assumes a uniform distribution over the set of all range queries, the average result is dominated by ranges with size $\Theta(m)$, where m is the total number of unit bins, since there are more of them.

- **Effect of randomness.** Algorithms that satisfy ϵ-DP are randomized, and thus the performance of any single run is randomized. This can be dealt with by using standard statistical techniques. For example, one can measure mean and standard deviation of error. Or one can show that the error will be below some threshold with probability of a certain value.

  There is another option in measuring the utility for range queries:

- **Absolute error or relative error.** The absolute error is the absolute difference between the noisy answer and the true answer. The impact of the same absolute error is different when the true answers are different. For example, a standard deviation of 5 may be perfectly acceptable if the true answer is 1,000, but totally unacceptable if the true answer is 1. The relative error addresses this limitation and is typically defined as the absolute error divided by the true answer. One potential problem is that sometimes the true answer may be very small, or even 0, in which case a very large relative error may not be meaningful. Typically one chooses a threshold θ to be used as the denominator if the true value is smaller than θ; that is

$$\text{relative error} = \frac{|\text{true answer} - \text{obtained answer}|}{\max(\theta, \text{true answer})}.$$

We will use the absolute error as the utility metric in this chapter.

4.2 DENSE PRE-DEFINED PARTITIONING

In this setting, we are given a pre-defined partitioning, and the average bin count is sufficiently high. While it is difficult to be precise about what we mean by "sufficiently high," a rule of thumb is that the average bin count is at least $\geq \frac{5}{\epsilon}$, by limiting the ratio between the average absolute Laplace noise which is $1/\epsilon$ and the average bin count to be $\leq 20\%$. We limit our attention to a one-dimensional dataset. While this is a very limited setting, the techniques developed here are basic building blocks for other settings.

The methods considered in this setting have the property that the errors are dataset-independent. Regarding query distribution, we can consider either the worst-case range query, or the uniform distribution over all range queries. We mostly consider the *Mean Absolute Error (MAE)*, which is the average of the absolute difference between the noisy answer and the true answer. This can be computed for a single query, where the randomness is from the noise added by the mechanism, or for a set of queries with a (typically uniform) probability distribution, where the randomness also comes from the choice of the query. In our analysis, we often use the *Mean Squared Absolute Error (MSAE)* as a substitute for MAE. They are highly correlated. MSAE is often easier to compute, as the MSAE for each query is the variance of the random noise.

4.2.1 THE BASELINE: A SIMPLE HISTOGRAM

The baseline approach is to apply the Laplacian mechanism to the histogram consisting of all unit bins, i.e., adding noises sampled from the $\mathsf{Lap}\left(\frac{1}{\epsilon}\right)$ distribution to each bin. This satisfies ϵ-DP under the unbounded DP interpretation, where adding/removing one tuple can affect at most one bin by 1. The noise added to each unit bin count has variance $\frac{2}{\epsilon^2}$; and we use

$$V_u = \frac{2}{\epsilon^2} \tag{4.1}$$

to denote this unit of variance. A range query r is answered by summing up the noisy counts of all unit bins included in the range. For a range query r, the MSAE, which equals the variance of the absolute error, is $\frac{2|r|}{\epsilon^2} = |r| \cdot V_u$, where $|r|$ is the number of bins included in the query, and the MAE is $\frac{\sqrt{|r|}}{\epsilon}$. Thus the worst-case MSAE is $\Theta(m)$, where m is the number of unit bins.

If we assume that the query distribution we are interested in is the uniform distribution over the set of all possible range queries, then the average length of all queries over m unit intervals is $\frac{\sum_{j=1}^{m} j(m-j+1)}{m(m+1)/2} = \frac{(m+2)}{3}$. Hence the average-case MSAE is $\frac{(m+2)}{3} V_u$. This is linear in the number of bins.

This baseline method works well with histograms that have a small number of unit bins. Indeed, when there are just a few bins, it appears that this method cannot be improved upon. When the number of unit bins is large, and when one cares about the absolute error, then this method becomes beatable. In particular, when answering range queries, the MASE increases linearly in the size of the query range.

We point out, however, that if one cares about **relative error** instead of absolute error, then this baseline method becomes hard to beat again. Roughly speaking, for queries regarding unit bins, this method performs the best. When the query size $|r|$ increases, the absolute error increases linearly in $\sqrt{|r|}$, and the denominator for computing the relative error, on average increases linearly in $|r|$. Thus, on average the relative error for larger queries tends to be become smaller as the query size increases. However, the worst-case relative error for this method may be high; this occurs when a query covers many bins, yet has a very low true count.

4.2.2   THE HIERARCHICAL METHOD

In the hierarchical method, in addition to publishing counts for unit bins, one also publishes counts for larger intervals. Conceptually, one can arrange all such published intervals into a tree, where the unit bins are the leaves, and each internal node in the tree corresponds to an interval that is the union of the intervals of its children. Let $h = \lceil \log_b m \rceil$, where b is the branching factor and m is the number of unit bins. This method can be viewed as publishing h different histograms of the data, each using a different granularity. Assuming that the privacy budget is divided equally among the histograms, the noise added to each counting query has variance $\frac{2h^2}{\epsilon^2} = h^2 V_u$. Given a range query, one finds the least number of nodes that correspond to the query range and sums up the noisy counts in the leaves. For example, in the tree illustrated in Figure 4.1, to answer the query $[v_2, v_5]$, one sums up the value of n_8, n_4, and n_{11}.

The benefit of this method is that any range query can be answered using no more than $2(b-1)h$ nodes in the tree (with at most $2(b-1)$ nodes in each level). The cost one has to pay is that the noise variance for each individual node is increased by a factor of h^2. The worst-case MSAE is thus $\Theta((\log m)^3)$, which is a significant asymptotic improvement compared with $\Theta(m)$ for the simple histogram method.

The branching factor b affects the accuracy in two ways. Increasing b reduces the height of the tree, thereby increasing the privacy budget available to each query, and improving the accuracy. At the same time, increasing b requires more nodes to be used to answer a query on average. To choose the optimal branching factor b, one needs to balance these two effects. The following theorem gives the formula for the MSAE.

Lemma 4.1   *[Qardaji et al. [2013a]] The method* $\mathbf{H}_b$ *has the following MSAE over the uniform distribution of all range queries with m unit bins:*

$$\text{MSAE}[\mathbf{H}_b] = \frac{m}{m+1}\left((b-1)h^3 - \frac{2(b+1)h^2}{3} + O\left(\frac{bh}{m}\right)\right)V_u. \tag{4.2}$$

See Qardaji et al. [2013a] for the proof, which is essentially an analysis of the average number of nodes that are included in any query.

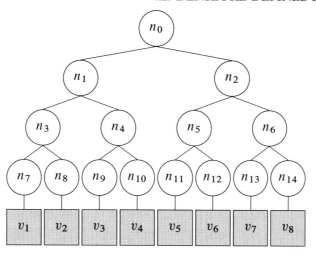

Figure 4.1: Effect of constrained inference. This figure demonstrates a hierarchical tree for $m = 8, b = 2$. We use n_i to denote the original noisy count for node i, and n'_i to denote the count after constrained inference. Then we have

$$
\begin{aligned}
n'_7 &= \tfrac{13}{21}n_7 + \tfrac{5}{21}n_3 + \tfrac{1}{7}n_1 - \tfrac{2}{21}n_4 - \tfrac{1}{21}(n_9 + n_{10}) - \tfrac{8}{21}n_8, \\
n'_8 &= \tfrac{13}{21}n_8 + \tfrac{5}{21}n_3 + \tfrac{1}{7}n_1 - \tfrac{2}{21}n_4 - \tfrac{1}{21}(n_9 + n_{10}) - \tfrac{8}{21}n_7, \\
n'_9 &= \tfrac{13}{21}n_9 + \tfrac{5}{21}n_4 + \tfrac{1}{7}n_1 - \tfrac{2}{21}n_3 - \tfrac{1}{21}(n_7 + n_8) - \tfrac{8}{21}n_{10}, \\
q &= \tfrac{3}{7}n_1 + \tfrac{8}{21}n_3 + + \tfrac{1}{21}n_4 + \tfrac{4}{21}(n_7 + n_8) + \tfrac{11}{21}n_9 - \tfrac{10}{21}n_{10},
\end{aligned}
$$

where $q = n'_7 + n'_8 + n'_9$ is the answer to the range query includes the first three leaf nodes; we have $\mathsf{Var}[q] = \tfrac{399}{441}\mathsf{V}_O$, which is significantly smaller than the $2\mathsf{V}_O$ needed before constrained inference (using $n_3 + n_9$), where V_O is the variance of the n_i's.

By dropping the $\tfrac{m}{m+1}$ factor and the $O(\tfrac{1}{m})$ term in Equation (4.2), we obtain the following approximation of $\mathsf{V}_{Avg}[\mathbf{H}_b]$, which we use $\mathsf{V}^*_{Avg}[\mathbf{H}_b]$ to denote:

$$
\mathsf{V}^*_{Avg}[\mathbf{H}_b] = \left((b-1)h^3 - \frac{2(b+1)h^2}{3} \right) \cdot \mathsf{V}_u. \tag{4.3}
$$

The above approximation can be understood as follows. On each level, the left end of the query may include $0, 1, \cdots, b-1$ nodes, which averages to $(b-1)/2$; similarly the right end of the query includes on average $(b-1)/2$. Thus on average a query needs to be answered by $(b-1)h$ nodes, where each node is answered with privacy budget $\tfrac{\epsilon}{h}$, and hence error variance of $h^2\mathsf{V}_u$. This explains the first and most significant term in Equation (4.3). The second term is due to the fact that some queries may not need all levels to answer it. For the binary case, we have

$$
\mathsf{V}^*_{Avg}[\mathbf{H_2}] = \left(h^3 - 2h^2 \right) \cdot \mathsf{V}_u. \tag{4.4}
$$

Optimal Branching Factor. The optimal branching factor b should minimize Equation (4.3). Because $h = \lceil \log_b m \rceil$ is not a continuous function, we cannot find a closed form solution for the value b. However, given any m, it is straightforward to computationally find the b value that minimizes Equation (4.3) by trying different b values.

Another use of Lemma 4.1 is to get a sense of what is the optimal branching factor for very large m values. When m is very large, we can use $\log_b m$ to approximate $\lceil \log_b m \rceil$. Trying to minimize $(b - 1) \left(\log_b m\right)^3 - \frac{2}{3}(b + 1) \left(\log_b m\right)^2$, however, results in b dependent on m. When m is very large, the first term $(b - 1) \left(\log_b m\right)^3$ dominates the second term, and we can choose b such that the first term's derivative, $\frac{-3b + b \log b + 3}{b \log^3 b} \log^3 m$, is 0. This results in $b \approx 16.8$. When setting $b = 16$, this results in MSAE reduction from $\mathbf{H_2}$ by a factor of approximately $\frac{(\log_2 16)^3}{(16 - 1)} \approx 4.27$.

4.2.3   CONSTRAINED INFERENCE

An important technique for differential privacy is that of constrained inference. The high-level intuition is that when many queries are asked for a given dataset, there may exist constraints that these answers should satisfy. However, since independent random noises are added, these constraints are often violated. By exploiting these constraints, it is possible to improve the accuracy of the random answers. In a trivial example, suppose that the same query is asked twice, with each answer obtained by adding Laplacian noise for satisfying $\left(\frac{\epsilon}{2}\right)$-DP, then exploiting the inherent constraint that the two answers should be the same, one could use the average of the two answers as a better answer for the query. Note that doing so does not violate DP, since it performs post-processing on answers obtained while satisfying DP. In this case, the average of two answers (each obtained with privacy budget $\left(\frac{\epsilon}{2}\right)$) to the same query is still less accurate than what one could get by asking the query once using ϵ as the privacy budget.

In the context of Hierarchical Histograms, query results at different levels should satisfy certain consistency constraints. More specifically, the count of each internal node should equal the total counts of all its children nodes. Exploiting these constraints can result in better answers to queries.

Consider the example in Figure 4.1. Given a query for range $[v_1, v_4]$, this can be answered directly by using the value at node n_1, but it can also be answered by summing up the values at node n_3 and n_4. When no noise is added, the two ways of answering should give the same result. When noises are added, however, the two ways may give two different answers. The key insight is that these two answers are two estimates of the true value, perturbed by *independently* generated noise. Intuitively, averaging over them will result in a more accurate answer than either.

Constrained inference here has two phases: weighted averaging, and mean consistency.

Weighted averaging. In this phase, one works from the leaf nodes all the way up to the root, updating every node with a count that is a weighted average of the node's original noisy count, and the sum of the total counts of the node's children. The weights are computed based on the following fact.

Lemma 4.2   *Given two random variables X_1 and X_2 that are both unbiased estimates of the same underlying quantity, then $X = \alpha X_1 + (1 - \alpha)X_2$ is also an unbiased estimate of the quantity, and the variance of X is minimized when $\alpha = \frac{\mathsf{Var}(X_2)}{\mathsf{Var}(X_1)+\mathsf{Var}(X_2)}$, at which point the variance of X is $\frac{\mathsf{Var}(X_1)\mathsf{Var}(X_2)}{\mathsf{Var}(X_1)+\mathsf{Var}(X_2)}$, less than $\min(\mathsf{Var}(X_1), \mathsf{Var}(X_2))$, and equals $\frac{\mathsf{Var}(X_1)}{2}$ when $\mathsf{Var}(X_1) = \mathsf{Var}(X_2)$.*

Let $n[v]$ be the noisy count for the node v which is at level i in the tree with branching factor b, where level 1 consists of leaf nodes. We use the weighted average of its original noisy count and the sum of its children's count to update the node's noisy count. The updated count $z_i[v]$ can be computed as:

$$
z_i[v] = \begin{cases} n[v], & \text{if } i = 1, \text{ i.e., } v \text{ is a leaf node,} \\ \frac{b^i - b^{i-1}}{b^i - 1} n[v] + \frac{b^{i-1} - 1}{b^i - 1} \sum_{u \in child(v)} z_{i-1}[u], & \text{if } i > 1. \end{cases}
$$

The intuition behind $z_i[v]$ is that it is a weighted average of two estimates for the count at v, where the weights are inversely proportional to the variance of the estimates. This reduces the error variance of each node.

Mean consistency.   In this phase, one works from the root down to the leaf level, updating each node count so that the sum of each node's children is the same as the node's count, improving the children nodes' accuracy in the process. Interestingly, this also ensures that each node is updated with the most accurate estimate. The mean consistency step aims at ensuring that for each node, its children values sum up to be the same as the parent. This is done by equally dividing the difference between the sum of the values of the children, and the value of the parent, among all the children, as follows, where u is the parent of v.

$$
\bar{n}_i[v] = \begin{cases} z_i[v], & \text{if } v \text{ is root,} \\ z_i[v] + \frac{1}{b}\left(\bar{n}_{i+1}[u] - \sum_{v \in child(u)} z_i[v]\right), & \text{ow.} \end{cases}
$$

After the two phases, the effect is such that each node v's value is a weighted sum of the original noisy counts of all nodes in the hierarchy. With nodes under v and nodes along the path from v to the root have positive weights, all other nodes have negative weights. Figure 4.1 gives an example showing the effect of constrained inference.

Effect of constrained inference.   An interesting question is how large is the noise reduction effect of the above constrained inferencing process. An analysis of this is provided in Qardaji et al. [2013a]. Approximately, one can reduce the variance (equivalently, MSAE) by a factor of 3. The analysis is quite involved, and interested readers are referred to Qardaji et al. [2013a].

4.2.4   EFFECT OF PRIVACY BUDGET ALLOCATION IN HIERARCHICAL HISTOGRAMS

Another optimization that affects the error of hierarchical histograms is the division of privacy budget among all the levels. The default choice is to divide the privacy budget evenly among all h levels. Some authors have suggested a geometrical allocation where each level has a privacy budget that is $\sqrt[3]{b}$ of its parent level, because each level has b times the number of nodes as the parent level. Intuitively, an optimal privacy budget allocation depends on the distribution of queries and should consider how much each level contributes to the total error variances for all queries, and then allocate privacy budget accordingly. This again depends on the branching factor, and whether the constrained inference optimization is used. An analysis of the interaction among these three factors, branching factor, constrained inference, and budget allocation, for the case where the queries of interest are uniformly selected from the set of all range queries, is carried out in Qardaji et al. [2013a]. The main conclusions are as follows:

- If one adapts the choice of privacy budget allocation to the branching factor and applies constrained inference, then a wide range of branching factors have very similar performances.

- If one chooses the optimal branching factor and combines it with constrained inference, then using the default equal privacy budget allocation performs as well as using the optimal budget allocation.

4.2.5   WAVELET TRANSFORMS AND OTHER OPTIMIZATIONS

We now discuss two other interesting techniques that can be applied to histogram publishing.

Wavelet Transformation. This approach is proposed in Xiao et al. [2011]. In it, one performs a discrete Haar wavelet transform of the hierarchical histogram, and then adds noises to the Haar coefficients. This method works only for the binary tree. Instead of publishing for each node v the sum of all leaf nodes under v, one publishes h_0, the average of all leaf nodes, and, for each non-leaf node v, the Harr coefficient $h_v = (a_\ell - a_r)/2$, where a_ℓ and a_r are, respectively, the average of all leaves in the left and right subtree of v. For each node v, knowing the average of all leaf nodes in the subtree rooted at v to be a, then using the coefficient h_v one can compute a_ℓ and a_r as $a_\ell = a + h_v$ and $a_r = a - h_v$. Thus, using these coefficients, one can reconstruct the counts of any node. An example of the discrete Harr wavelet transformation is illustrated in Figure 4.2. For example, if we want to reconstruct the count of v_3, we find the path from h_0 to v_3, and obtained $v_4 = h_0 - h_1 + h_4 = 5 - 1 + 2 = 6$.

When a range query r is answered, one sums up all leaf nodes, which becomes a weighted sum of the noisy Harr coefficients. If any node is fully contained in a query, then the coefficients for that node and all nodes in the subtree are not needed, since one needs only to know the average counts of all leaf nodes in the subtree, and does not need to know how these counts are distributed within the tree.

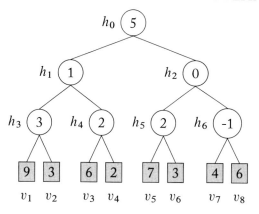

Figure 4.2: Example of discrete Harr wavelet transformation.

In terms of utility, applying the Wavelet transform is similar to the effect of conducting constrained optimization on a binary tree, and does not perform as well as combining an optimal branching factor (e.g., 16) with constrained inference. While mathematically interesting, this technique offers no utility advantage because the cancelling effect it exploits is specific to a binary tree, and it cannot be combined with a hierarchy of branching factors other than 2.

The Matrix Mechanism. The concept of the Matrix mechanism was originally proposed in Li et al. [2010]. It optimizes for a workload of counting queries. Since each counting query can be represented as a binary vector that selects the unit bins included in the query, a set of queries can be represented as a matrix. Given such a matrix, one can find an alternative set of queries, called a query strategy. Standard Laplace noise is then added to the strategy queries, the answers to which are used to derive answers to the original workload. The goal is thus finding the best query strategy in order to answer the given workload queries with minimum error. This problem can be expressed as a semi-definite optimization problem. Unfortunately, given a query workload on a histogram of m unit bins, solving the optimization problem requires time complexity $O(m^6)$. For the range of m that can be solved in this exact method, the best method is the flat histogram method. Some approximation mechanisms have been developed [Li and Miklau, 2012, Yuan et al., 2012]. They have time complexity $O(m^3)$, which still does not scale for large m's. Furthermore, because these are approximations, they produce worse results than the hierarchical histogram methods.

While the Matrix mechanism can be claimed to be general in the sense that it can be applied to any set of workload queries, for the case of publishing histograms, it is actually less general than other methods. For the other methods, one obtains a general method that can be applied for any value of m. For the Matrix mechanism, however, one has to perform the computation for every individual m value.

4.2.6 BEYOND ONE-DIMENSIONAL DATASETS

The idea of using hierarchy with constrained inference can be applied to higher dimensions. However, the benefit of using hierarchies quickly disappears as the number of dimensions increases. Let d be the number of dimensions, n be the number of unit bins for each dimension, and $m = n^d$ denote the total number of bins. For the 1D case, using the hierarchical method reduces worst-case MSAE from $2m$ to $2(b-1)\lceil \log_b m \rceil^3$. For the two-dimensional (2D) case, the MSAE is $b(\sqrt{m}-1)\lceil \log_{b^2} m \rceil^2$, which includes a $\sqrt{m}$ factor. Asymptotically, the MSAE is $\Theta(m^{(d-1)/d})$, a number that is increasingly close to m as d increases. More concretely, it is found that the simple histogram method outperforms all hierarchical methods for $m < 45$ for the 1D case, $m < 4096$ for the 2D case, and $m < 1.7E9$ for 3D, and $m < 2.18E9$ for 4D. We note that when the number of unit bins gets close to (or is larger than) the number of tuples of a dataset, the true counts tend to be overwhelmed by the added noises.

The curse of dimensionality in the case of k-anonymity is known [Aggarwal, 2005]; this is a similar effect for DP. The reason behind this effect is that when using the hierarchy to answer a large query, one gains significantly for the portion answered using an internal node, but still needs to use leaf nodes to obtain answers for the border regions. In the 1D case, a "border" of constant width has a volume that is $\Theta(\frac{1}{m})$ of the total domain, whereas in the 2D case, a "border" of constant width occupies a volume that is $\Theta(\frac{1}{\sqrt{m}})$ of the total domain. The higher the dimension, the larger the percentage a "border" of constant width would occupy.

4.3 LACKING SUITABLE PARTITIONING

We now consider the case that a suitable partitioning does not exist, that is, it does not make sense to publish all unit bin counts. One situation in which this may be the case is when there exists a pre-defined partitioning, but the average number of data points for each bin is low. If one publishes the unit bin counts, the added noises likely overwhelm the true counts for most bins. Another situation is when the number of natural unit bins is so large that it is infeasible to enumerate through all of them. For example, this will be the case when the data values are real numbers, and the natural bins correspond to the precision of the real number that one cares about.

In either situation, one will need to publish a histogram such that the unit bins are of a more coarse granularity than the input data. That is, the queries one asks may include only part of some unit bins. There are thus two sources of errors when answering a query.

The **noise error** is due to the fact that the bin counts are noisy. When summing up the noisy counts of q bins to answer a query, the resulting noise error is the sum of the corresponding noises. As these noises are independently generated zero-mean random variables, they cancel each other out to a certain degree so that the variance of their sum equals the sum of their variances. That is, the noise error of a query grows linearly in $\sqrt{q}$. Therefore, the finer granularity one partitions the domain into, the more cells are included in a query, and the larger the noise error is.

The **non-uniformity error** is caused by bins that intersect with the query, but are not contained in it. For these bins, we need to estimate how many data points are in the intersection assuming that the data points are distributed uniformly. This estimation will have errors when the data points are not distributed uniformly. The magnitude of the non-uniformity error in any intersected bin, in general, depends on the number of data points in that bin, and is bounded by it. Therefore, the finer the partition granularity, the lower the non-uniformity error.

As argued above, reducing the noise error and non-uniformity error imposes conflicting demands on the partition granularity. The main challenge of partition-based differentially private synopsis lies in how to meet this challenge and reconcile the conflicting needs of noise error and non-uniformity error.

4.3.1 THE UNIFORM GRID METHOD—UG

One simple approach is the Uniform Grid (UG) method. This approach partitions the data domain into M grid cells of equal size, and then obtains a noisy count for each cell. The accuracy of UG is highly dependent on the grid size M. In Qardaji et al. [2013b], the following guideline is offered for choosing m which minimizes the sum of the two kinds of errors.

Guideline To minimize the errors of UG in a two-dimensional dataset, the grid size should be about

$$\sqrt{\frac{N\epsilon}{c}}, \tag{4.5}$$

where N is the number of data points, ϵ is the total privacy budget, and c is some small constant depending on the dataset.

Below we present the analysis supporting this guideline. As the sensitivity of the count query is 1, the noise added for each cell follows the distribution $\mathsf{Lap}\left(\frac{1}{\epsilon}\right)$ and has a standard deviation of $\frac{\sqrt{2}}{\epsilon}$. Given an $m \times m$ grid, and a query that selects r portion of the domain (where r is the ratio of the area of the query rectangle to the area of the whole domain), about rm^2 cells are included in the query, and the total noise error thus has standard deviation of $\frac{\sqrt{2rm^2}}{\epsilon} = \frac{\sqrt{2r}m}{\epsilon}$.

The non-uniformity error is proportional to the number of data points in the cells that fall on the border of the query rectangle. For a query that selects r portion of the domain, it has four edges, whose lengths are proportional to $\sqrt{r}$ of the domain length; thus the query's border contains on the order of $\sqrt{r}m$ cells, which on average includes on the order of $\sqrt{r}m \times \frac{N}{m^2} = \frac{\sqrt{r}N}{m}$ data points. Assuming that the non-uniformity error on average is some portion of the total density of the cells on the query border, then the non-uniformity error is $\frac{\sqrt{r}N}{c_0 m}$ for some constant c_0. We can equate the standard deviation of the non-uniformity error with this. To minimize the two errors' sum, $\frac{\sqrt{2r}m}{\epsilon} + \frac{\sqrt{r}N}{mc_0}$, we should set m to $\sqrt{\frac{N\epsilon}{c}}$, where $c = \sqrt{2}c_0$.

Using the guideline requires knowing N, the number of data points. Obtaining a noisy estimate of N using a very small portion of the total privacy budget suffices.

The parameter c depends on the uniformity of the dataset. In the extreme case where the dataset is completely uniform, then the optimal grid size is 1×1. That is, the best method is to obtain as accurate a total count as possible, and then any query can be fairly accurately answered by computing what fraction of the region is covered by the query. This corresponds to a large c. When a dataset is highly non-uniform, then a smaller c value is desirable. $c = 10$ is suggested by Qardaji et al. [2013b].

4.3.2   THE ADAPTIVE GRIDS APPROACH—AG, 2D CASE

The main disadvantage of UG is that it treats all regions in the dataset equally. That is, both dense and sparse regions are partitioned in exactly the same way. This is not optimal. If a region has very few points, this method might result in *over*-partitioning of the region, creating a set of cells with close to zero data points. This has the effect of increasing the noise error with little reduction in the non-uniformity error. On the other hand, if a region is very dense, this method might result in *under*-partitioning of the region. As a result, the non-uniformity error would be quite large.

Ideally, when a region is dense, we want to use finer granularity partitioning, because the non-uniformity error in this region greatly outweighs that of noise error. Similarly, when a region is sparse (having few data points), we want to use a more coarse grid there. Based on this observation, we propose an Adaptive Grids (AG) approach.

The AG approach works as follows. We first lay a coarse $m_1 \times m_1$ grid over the data domain, creating $(m_1)^2$ first-level cells, and then we issue a count query for each cell using a privacy budget $\alpha\epsilon$, where $0 < \alpha < 1$. For each cell, let N' be the noisy count of the cell, AG then partitions the cell using a grid size that is adaptively chosen based on N', creating leaf cells. The parameter α determines how to split the privacy budget between the two levels.

Applying Constrained Inference.   Let v be the noisy count of a first-level cell, and let $u_{1,1}, \ldots, u_{m_2,m_2}$ be the noisy counts of the cells that v is further partitioned into in the second level. One can then apply constrained inference as follows. First, one obtains a more accurate count v' by taking the weighted average of v and the sum of $u_{i,j}$ such that the standard deviation of the noise error at v' is minimized.

$$v' = \frac{\alpha^2 m_2^2}{(1-\alpha)^2 + \alpha^2 m_2^2} v + \frac{(1-\alpha)^2}{(1-\alpha)^2 + \alpha^2 m_2^2} \sum u_{i,j}.$$

This value is then propagated to the leaf nodes by distributing the difference among all nodes equally

$$u'_{i,j} = u_{i,j} + \left(v' - \sum u_{i,j} \right).$$

When $m_2 = 1$, the constrained inference step becomes issuing another query with budget $(1 - \alpha)\epsilon$ and then computing a weighted average of the two noisy counts.

Choosing Parameters for AG. The selection of the grid size for each first-level cell is suggested by the following guideline.

Guideline Given a cell with a noisy count of N', to minimize the errors, this cell should be partitioned into $m_2 \times m_2$ cells, where m_2 is computed as follows:

$$\left\lceil \sqrt{\frac{N'(1-\alpha)\epsilon}{c_2}} \right\rceil, \tag{4.6}$$

where $(1 - \alpha)\epsilon$ is the remaining privacy budget for obtaining noisy counts for leaf cells, $c_2 = c/2$, and c is the same constant as in guideline for UG.

The analysis to support this guideline is as follows. When the first-level cell is further partitioned into $m_2 \times m_2$ leaf cells, only queries whose borders go through this first-level cell will be affected. These queries may include $0, 1, 2, \cdots$, up to $m_2 - 1$ rows (or columns) of leaf cells, and thus $0, m_2, 2m_2, \cdots, (m_2 - 1)m_2$ leaf cells. When a query includes more than half of these leaf cells, constrained inference has the effect that the query is answered using the count obtained in the first level cell minus those leaf cells that are not included in the query. Therefore, on average a query is answered using

$$\frac{1}{m_2} \left(\sum_{i=0}^{m_2-1} \min(i, m_2 - i) \right) m_2 \approx \frac{(m_2)^2}{4}$$

leaf cells, and the average noise error is on the order of $\sqrt{\frac{(m_2)^2}{4}} \frac{\sqrt{2}}{(1-\alpha)\epsilon}$. The average non-uniformity error is about $\frac{N'}{c_0 m_2}$; therefore to minimize their sum, we should choose m_2 to be about $\sqrt{\frac{N'(1-\alpha)\epsilon}{\sqrt{2}c_0/2}}$.

The choice of m_1, the grid-size for the first level, is less critical than the choice of m_2. When m_1 is larger, the average density of each cell is smaller, and the further partitioning step will partition each cell into fewer numbers of cells. When m_1 is smaller, the further partitioning step will partition each cell into more cells. In general, m_1 should be less than the grid size for UG computed according to Guideline 4.5, since it will further partition each cell. At the same time, m_1 should not be too small either. We set

$$m_1 = \max\left(10, \frac{1}{4}\left\lceil \sqrt{\frac{N\epsilon}{c}} \right\rceil\right).$$

The choice of α also appears to be less critical. Qardaji et al. [2013b] suggested that setting α to be in the range of $[0.2, 0.6]$ results in similar accuracy.

Summary In Qardaji et al. [2013b], a detailed study and comparison of the above methods, evaluated on four real datasets, including large geo-spatial datasets, is reported, and MRE is used as the main metric. Methodology for choosing grid size for UG and parameters for AG is proposed. The evaluation shows that AG outperform the other approaches.

4.3.3   BOTTOM-UP GROUPING

A number of techniques have been developed to deal with the case where there exists a pre-defined partitioning and m, the number of unit bins, is not so large that running time in $\Theta(m)$ is unacceptable. A key challenge is that coming up with a partitioning may involve many decisions (e.g., the number of bins). If one makes each such decision differentially private, then one has to divide the privacy budget up very finely, resulting in poor partitioning. We now discuss some of these methods.

The NoisyFirst method, proposed in Xu et al. [2012], first computes a flat noisy histogram, and then merges bins on the noisy data to reduce the error. It uses dynamic programming to compute a merging of these noisy counts so that the sum of squared errors (SSE) is minimized. This method is mostly for one-dimensional datasets. Since we are optimizing based on the noisy counts (instead of the true counts), it is unclear whether optimizing the SSE is the best choice. We conjecture that an alternative merging strategy that merges adjacent cells that have counts below a certain threshold (so that they are likely caused by cells of very low counts) would produce a better result. We also note that if the goal is to reduce noise error from cells that have low counts, it is unnecessary to merge adjacent cells, and one could skip cells that have large counts when merging. This avoids non-uniformity errors.

The StructureFirst method [Xu et al., 2012] uses half of the privacy budget to get the structure that fits the data and noise well, and spends another half of the privacy budget on releasing a histogram with Laplace mechanism based on the chosen structure. To find a good structure, the StructureFirst iteratively chooses the right boundary of histogram bins using exponential mechanism with a score function computing the expected error of histogram merged by each right boundary. For k, the number of bins after merging, an empirical choice that $k = |H|/10$, where $|H|$ denotes number of bins in the histogram, is suggested. We note that this method requires making k decisions, and the privacy budget $\epsilon/2$ must be divided into k portions. Since typically k is quite large, this likely results in poor choices, because very little privacy budget for each choice is allocated.

The DAWA (Data-Aware and Workload-Aware) algorithm [Li et al., 2014a] also attempts to select a partitioning that optimizes the balance between the noise error and the non-uniformity error. A cost function that estimates the combined effects of these two sources of errors is introduced. One first computes this cost for each possible interval, and adds a certain noise to this cost. One then uses a dynamic programming method to select the combination of intervals that has the lowest noisy cost.

In Rastogi and Nath [2010], it is proposed that one applies the Discrete Fourier Transform (DFT) to the histogram, and then perturbs the first k elements of the Fourier coefficients. The intuition is that while applying the Laplace mechanism directly on n queries results in a noise of $\Theta(n)$, perturbing the first k element after Discrete Fourier Transform improves the expected error to roughly $\Theta(k)$. One then uses the noisy version of k Fourier coefficients to reconstruct all n query answers. In particular, instead of applying Laplace mechanism with L1 sensitivity Δ_1 on original queries, Rastogi and Nath [2010] proves that one can apply Laplace mechanism on Fourier coefficients with L1 sensitivity at most $\sqrt{k}$ times the L2 sensitivity of query, i.e., $\sqrt{k}\Delta_2$. As pointed out in Rastogi and Nath [2010], one can further use a differentially private sampling algorithm, based on estimating the tradeoff between reconstruction error and perturbation error, to determine k before applying perturbation on Discrete Fourier Transform.

An improvement proposed in Acs et al. [2012] considers two aspects: a new score function for selecting k with better accuracy, and the coefficients of DFT for real-valued histograms are correlated. Specifically, Acs et al. [2012] proves a better bound for expected error between the original histogram and the noisy histogram, with the bound only depending on parameter k, instead of $k\sqrt{n}$ in Rastogi and Nath [2010]. In addition, Acs et al. [2012] explains that the coefficients of real-valued histograms are half-redundant (i.e., $\hat{F}_i = \hat{F}^*_{n-i}$ for $1 \leq i \leq (n-1)/2$). Based on this fact, Acs et al. [2012] considers the candidates of k only between 1 to $(n+1)/2$, instead of 1 to n in Rastogi and Nath [2010].

These DFT-based methods can be effective when the data distribution is smooth, so that it can be well approximated using the first few DFT terms. When the data are not smooth, they perform worse than methods such as **AG**.

4.3.4   RECURSIVE PARTITIONING

Several methods perform recursive partitioning of the data domain.

In Xiao et al. [2010], it is proposed to adapt the standard spatial indexing method, KD-trees. Nodes in a KD-tree are recursively split along some dimension. In order to minimize the non-uniformity error, Xiao et al. [2010] use the heuristic to choose the split point such that the two sub-regions are as close to uniform as possible. In addition, they implemented a two-step algorithm that first generates synthetic data based on a uniform partitioning of the data domain, and then generates the KD-tree partitions based on the synthetic data.

In Cormode et al. [2012], several alternatives based on KD-trees are introduced. Instead of using a uniformity heuristic, they split the nodes along the median of the partition dimension. The height of the tree is predetermined and the privacy budget is divided among the levels. Part of the privacy budget is used to choose the median, and part is used to obtain the noisy count.

Cormode et al. [2012] also proposed a quad-tree based approach, in which nodes are recursively divided into four equal regions via horizontal and vertical lines through the midpoint of each range. That is, no privacy budget is used to decide how to partition. This partitioning is repeated for a predetermined number of levels. Another approach in Cormode et al. [2012] combines the aforementioned two approaches, which they call "KD-hybrid." This method uses a quadtree for the first few levels of partitions, and then uses the KD-tree approach for the other levels. A number of other optimizations were also applied in all their techniques, including the constrained inference presented in Hay et al. [2010], and optimized allocation of a privacy budget.

Qardaji and Li [2012] proposed a general recursive partitioning framework for multidimensional datasets. At each level of recursion, partitioning is performed along the dimension which results in the most balanced partitioning of the data points. The balanced partitioning employed by this method has the effect of producing regions of similar size. When applied to two-dimensional datasets, this approach is very similar to building a KD-tree based on noisy median.

Another similar approach is P-HPartition in Acs et al. [2012], which also uses the exponential mechanism to iteratively bisect the data domain. The quality function considers both the reconstruction error (i.e., the non-uniformity error) and noise error.

Recursive partitioning requires many steps to arrive at the final partitioning. This created two problems. The first is that the privacy budget must be divided into many portions, so that each individual selection may not have a sufficient privacy budget to make an accurate selection. The second is that this is a greedy approach. In each iteration, the algorithm is making a decision that is at best locally optimal. Even without adding noises to satisfy DP, combining these locally optimal choices may be sub-optimal globally.

4.4   BIBLIOGRAPHICAL NOTES

See Hay et al. [2016], Qardaji et al. [2013a,b] for experimental evaluation and analysis of these methods. It is found that among data-independent methods, Hierarchical Histograms with constrained inferencing and a large branching factor performs the best, and AG and DAWA are the two best-performing algorithms among the data-dependent methods.

Hay et al. [2010] introduced the hierarchical method and constrained inferences for the binary case. These are extended to a tree of a branching factor b in Qardaji et al. [2013a]. The UG and AG method are introduced in Qardaji et al. [2013b]. The DAWA method is introduced in Li et al. [2014a].

CHAPTER 5

Differentially Private Optimization

Many data mining and machine learning problems can be viewed as optimization problems. Examples include k-means clustering, regression, and classification. We use D to denote the input dataset, ω_* to denote the desired output, and $J(D, \omega)$ to denote the objective function to be minimized. That is, we want to output

$$\omega_* = \underset{\omega}{\mathrm{argmin}}\, J(D, \omega).$$

Several interesting techniques have been developed to perform these optimization tasks while satisfying DP. In this chapter, we group these techniques into the following categories.

1. **Output Perturbation.** One method is to directly perturb the output of the optimization problem. This requires analyzing the sensitivity of the optimization problem; that is, how much ω_* changes when the input dataset D changes by one tuple. Unfortunately, the sensitivities of these optimization problems tend to be so high that such output perturbation destroys utility.

2. **Objective Perturbation.** There exists a class of methods unique to optimization problems. Instead of perturbing the output of the optimization problem, one can perturb the optimization objective function $J(D, \omega)$ to get $J^*(D, \omega)$ in a way such that optimizing according to $J^*(D, \omega)$ is differentially private.

3. **Making Existing Algorithms Private.** A second method is to take an existing optimization algorithm and make each individual step that needs access to the input dataset private.

4. **Iterative Local Search.** Another method is to perform an iterative local search to approach ω_*. In each iteration, given the current candidate or candidates, we can generate a pool of new candidates and use the exponential mechanism to select among them.

5. **Publishing Histograms for Optimization.** Finally, one can publish a histogram of D optimized for the purpose of the task, e.g., for clustering or for classification, and then perform optimization using the histogram. Intuitively, this publishes more information than needed for outputting ω_*; however, this appears to outperform the above methods in experiments.

5.1   EXAMPLE OPTIMIZATION PROBLEMS

We now give a brief description of the optimization problems that have been studied in the context of differential privacy, and discuss the feasibility of performing output perturbation for each of them.

5.1.1 k-MEANS CLUSTERING

k-means clustering is a widely used unsupervised machine learning method for data analysis. It has a wide range of applications, including but not limited to nearest neighbor queries, market segment, image processing, and geo-statistics.

The input is a dataset $D = \{x^1, x^2, \ldots, x^N\}$, where each data point x^ℓ is a d-dimensional real vector. Intuitively, the dataset D consists of points in a d-dimensional space. The output is a set of k points $\omega = \{o^1, o^2, \cdots, o^k\}$, known as the centroids. These k centroids partition D into k clusters such that each data point belongs to the cluster defined by the centroid that is closest to the data point. (If there are more than one closest centroid for a data point, the data point is assigned to one of the corresponding clusters.) The objective function to be minimized is the within-cluster sum of squares. We normalize this value and call it Normalized Intra-Cluster Variance (NICV), defined as follows.

$$J_{km}(D, \omega) = \frac{1}{N} \sum_{\ell=1}^{N} \min_{j=1}^{k} ||x^\ell - o^j||^2. \tag{5.1}$$

The standard k-means algorithm is the Lloyd's algorithm [Lloyd, 1982]. The algorithm starts by selecting k points as the initial choices for the centroid, and then tries to improve these centroid choices iteratively until no improvement can be made. In each iteration, one first uses the current centroid choices to partition the data points into k clusters $\mathbf{O} = \{O^1, O^2, \cdots, O^k\}$, with each point assigned to the same cluster as the nearest centroid. Then, one updates each centroid to be the center of the data points in the cluster.

$$\forall i \in [1..d] \; \forall j \in [1..k] \; o_i^j \leftarrow \frac{\sum_{x^\ell \in O^j} x_i^\ell}{|O^j|}, \tag{5.2}$$

where x_i^ℓ and o_i^j are the i-th dimension coordinates of x^ℓ and o^j, respectively. The algorithm continues by alternating between data partition and centroid update, until it converges.

The quality of the output computed by the Lloyd's algorithm is subject to the choice of the starting points. `Random Partition` and `Forgy` are two commonly adopted initialization methods. The former randomly partitions the database into k clusters, and takes the centers of the clusters as starting points. The latter randomly selects k data points (seeds) from the database as the starting points. One can run the algorithm multiple times, with different choices of initial centroids, and choose the output that has the minimal NICV.

The global sensitivity of the k-means clustering problem is very high, as changing one single data point could completely change the optimal clustering centroids; see Nissim et al. [2007].

5.1.2   LINEAR REGRESSION

Linear regression is a fundamental statistical approach for modeling the linear relationship between a dependent variable and several independent variables. It has been used extensively in practical applications, including fitting prediction models and analyzing the relationship between a dependent variable and one or more independent variables.

The input is a dataset $D = \{\langle x^1, y^1 \rangle, \langle x^2, y^2 \rangle, \ldots, \langle x^N, y^N \rangle\}$, where x^ℓ is a d-dimensional real vector, and y^ℓ is a real scalar value. The output is a d-dimensional vector ω. The optimization objective is

$$J_{\mathrm{lr}}(D, \omega) = \frac{1}{N} \sum_{\ell=1}^{N} \left(y^\ell - \sum_{i=1}^{d} x_i^\ell \omega_i \right)^2. \tag{5.3}$$

In other words, linear regression expresses the value of y as a linear function of the values of $x_1, \ldots, x_d$, such that the sum of square errors of the predicted y values is minimized.

The global sensitivity of linear regression is unbounded. For example, given a dataset where each x is one-dimensional with $N - 1$ points at $(0, 0)$ and 1 point at $(1/N, 0)$. The optimal line $y = 0\dot{x} + 0$. Adding an additional point $(1, N)$ to the input dataset results in an optimal line $y = N\dot{x} + 0$. Thus, adding noise to the line parameter according to the global sensitivity removes all utilities completely.

5.1.3   LOGISTIC REGRESSION

Logistic regression also learns a vector of linear coefficients; however, the inner product of these coefficients and a data point's independent variables is used to estimate the probability of the dependent variable, using the logistic function.

The input is a dataset $D = \{\langle x^1, y^1 \rangle, \langle x^2, y^2 \rangle, \ldots, \langle x^N, y^N \rangle\}$, where x^ℓ is a d-dimensional real vector, and y^ℓ has a boolean domain $\{0, 1\}$. The output is a prediction function, which predicts $y = 1$ with probability

$$\rho(\omega_*, x) = \frac{\exp(\omega_*^T x)}{1 + \exp(\omega_*^T x)}.$$

The model parameter ω_* is computed by minimizing the optimization objective function,

$$J_{log}(D, \omega) = \frac{\Lambda}{2} \|\omega\| + \frac{1}{N} \sum_{\ell=1}^{N} L_\omega(x^\ell, y),$$

where the loss function is defined as

$$L_\omega(x, y) = -y \log(\rho(\omega, x)) - (1 - y) \log(1 - \rho(\omega, x)),$$

and Λ is the regularization parameter.

In Chaudhuri and Monteleoni [2008], it is shown that the sensitivity of the output pertur-bation approach on logistic regression is $\frac{2}{N\Lambda}$, where Λ is the regularization parameter and N is the dataset size. Note that this means this bound becomes ∞ when no regularization is used.

5.1.4   SVM

Another widely used classification technique is support vector machine (SVM). It has promis-ing empirical performance in many practical applications, and especially works well with high-dimensional data. Given a set of training examples, each marked for belonging to one of two categories, an SVM training algorithm builds a model that assigns new examples into one cat-egory or the other, making it a non-probabilistic binary linear classifier. An SVM model is a representation of the examples as points in space, mapped so that the examples of the separate categories are divided by a clear gap that is as wide as possible.

The input is a dataset $D = \{\langle x^1, y^1 \rangle, \langle x^2, y^2 \rangle, \ldots, \langle x^N, y^N \rangle\}$, where x^ℓ is a d-dimensional real vector, and y^ℓ has a boolean domain $\{0, 1\}$. The output is a prediction function,

$$\rho(x) = \begin{cases} 1 & \text{if } \alpha_*^T \cdot x + \beta_* > 0 \\ 0 & \text{otherwise,} \end{cases}$$

where $\alpha_* \in \mathbb{R}^d$ and $\beta_* \in \mathbb{R}$ is computed by minimizing the optimization objective function,

$$J_{svm}(D, \alpha, \beta) = \frac{\Lambda}{2} \|\alpha\|^2 + \frac{1}{N} \sum_{\ell=1}^{N} L_{\alpha,\beta}(x^\ell, y^\ell),$$

where the loss function $L_{\alpha,\beta}(x, y)$ is defined as

$$L_{\alpha,\beta}(x, y) = \max\{1 - 4(y - 0.5)(\alpha^T x + \beta - 0.5), 0\},$$

and Λ is the regularization parameter.

Rubinstein et al. [2012] used the same approach for perturbing the parameters outputed by the SVM classifier and showed that the sensivitiy of the SVM learning algorithm can be bounded by $\frac{4L\Lambda\kappa\sqrt{d}}{N}$, where Λ is the regularization parameter, L is the Lipschitz constant of loss function, κ is the bound of kernel, d is dataset dimensionality, and N is the dataset size.

5.2   OBJECTIVE PERTURBATION

We have seen that the global sensitivities of these optimization problems are very high, mak-ing direct output perturbation an ineffective method. An interesting approach, first introduced in Chaudhuri and Monteleoni [2008], is to perturb the optimization objective function so that solving it results in a private solution. We now discuss two such techniques.

5.2.1 ADDING A NOISY LINEAR TERM TO THE OPTIMIZATION OBJECTIVE FUNCTION

One method, proposed in Chaudhuri and Monteleoni [2008], Chaudhuri et al. [2011], is to add a Laplacian noise to the optimization objective function. We want to solve

$$\underset{\omega}{\operatorname{argmin}} J(D, \omega), \text{ where } J(D, \omega) = \left(\frac{1}{N} \sum_{i=1}^{N} L(\omega, x_i)\right) + c(\omega),$$

where $c(\omega)$ is the regularizer.

Assuming that both $L(\omega, x_i)$ and $c(\omega)$ are strictly convex and everywhere differentiable for ω. Then define the new objective function to be

$$J^*(D, \omega) = J(D, \omega) + \frac{b^T \omega}{N},$$

where b is a random noise sampled from a distribution with density $\frac{1}{\alpha} e^{-\beta \|b\|}$, α is a normalizing constant, and β is a function of ϵ.

The privacy of this method is proved as follows.

Proposition 5.1   *Solving* $\operatorname{argmin}_\omega J^*(D, \omega)$ *satisfies* ϵ-DP.

Proof. Suppose we have any two neighboring datasets $D = (x_1, y_1), \ldots, (x_{N-1}, y_{N-1}), (a, y)$ and $D' = (x_1, y_1), \ldots, (x_{N-1}, y_{N-1})$. For any ω^* output by our algorithm, we want to show that

$$\frac{\Pr[\omega^*|D]}{\Pr[\omega^*|D']} \leq e^\epsilon.$$

Since the regularization function J and the loss function L are strictly convex and differentiable everywhere, a unique minimum occurs when the gradient of $J^*(D, \omega) = J(D, \omega) + \frac{b^T \omega}{n}$ is 0. Therefore, for the two neighboring datasets D and D', there are unique values of noise b that map the different inputs to the same output ω^*.

Let the values of b for the first and second cases respectively, be b_1 and b_2. We have

$$\frac{\partial J(D, \omega)}{\partial \omega} + \frac{b_1}{n} = \frac{\partial J(D', \omega)}{\partial \omega} + \frac{b_2}{n}.$$

Therefore,

$$
\begin{aligned}
\|b_1 - b_2\| &= \left\| \frac{\partial J(D, \omega)}{\partial \omega} - \frac{\partial J(D', \omega)}{\partial \omega} \right\| \\
&= \left\| \frac{\partial L(\omega, (a, y))}{\partial \omega} - \frac{\partial L(\omega, (a', y'))}{\partial \omega} \right\| \\
&\leq \Delta.
\end{aligned}
$$

And Δ is the sensitivity of $\frac{\partial J(D,\omega)}{\partial \omega}$.

Finally, we have,

$$\frac{\Pr[\omega^*|D]}{\Pr[\omega^*|D']} = \frac{\text{pdf}(b_1)}{\text{pdf}(b_2)} \leq e^{\frac{\epsilon}{\Delta} \cdot \|b_1 - b_2\|} \leq e^{\epsilon}.$$

$\square$

Chaudhuri and Monteleoni [2008], Chaudhuri et al. [2011] showed that $\Delta \leq 2$ for both logistic regression and SVM. The loss function of logistic regression is differentiable and can be bounded by 1, Therefore,

$$\|b_1 - b_2\| = \left\| \frac{\partial J(D,\omega)}{\partial \omega} - \frac{\partial J(D',\omega)}{\partial \omega} \right\|$$
$$\leq \left\| \frac{\partial L(\omega,(a,y))}{\partial \omega} \right\| + \left\| \frac{\partial L(\omega,(a',y'))}{\partial \omega} \right\|$$
$$\leq 2.$$

Although the loss function of SVM, $L_\omega(x,y) = \max\{1 - y(\alpha^T x + \beta), 0\}$, is not differentiable, Chaudhuri et al. [2011] proposed to use a differentiable version of this loss function, and showed that its first order derivative can be bounded by 1 and the noise scale can be bounded by 2.

It is difficult to analyze the impact of adding such linear terms to the objective function on the accuracy of the optimization results; however, experimental results show that this method is not very promising.

5.2.2 THE FUNCTIONAL MECHANISM

In Zhang et al. [2012], it is proposed to perturb the optimization objective function by first approximating the objective function using a polynomial, and then perturbing each and every coefficient of the polynomial.

Given an objective function $J(D,\omega) = \sum_{t_i \in D} L(t_i,\omega)$, the function mechanism first decomposes $J(D,\omega)$ into a series of polynomial bases,

$$J(D,\omega) = \sum_{j=0}^{U} \sum_{\phi \in \Phi_j} \sum_{t_i \in D} \lambda_{\phi t_i} \phi(\omega),$$

and then perturbs the aggregated coefficients of each polynomial basis with Laplace noise. In the above, D is the dataset, t_i is the i-th tuple in the dataset, and ω is the model parameter. And $\Phi_j (j \in \mathbb{N})$ denote the set of all products of parameter ω's coordinates $\{\omega_1, \ldots, \omega_d\}$ with degree j,

$$\Phi_j = \{\omega_1^{c_1} \omega_2^{c_d} \cdots \omega_d^{c_d} \mid \sum_{l=1}^{d} c_l = j\}.$$

For example, $\Phi_0 = \{1\}$, $\Phi_1 = \{\omega_1, \ldots, \omega_d\}$, and $\Phi_2 = \{\omega_i \cdot \omega_j | i, j \in [1, d]\}$.

Algorithm 5.1 Functional Mechanism

INPUT D: Dataset, $J(D, \omega)$: objective function, ϵ: privacy parameter

Output ω_*: best parameter vector

 Set $\Delta = 2 \max_t \sum_{j=1}^{U} \sum_{\phi \in \Phi_j} \|\lambda_{\phi t}\|_1$

 for each $0 \leq j \leq U$ **do**

   for each $\phi \in \Phi_j$ **do**

     set $\lambda_\phi = \sum_{t_i \in D} \lambda_{\phi t_i} + \text{Lap}\left(\frac{\Delta}{\epsilon}\right)$

   end for

 end for

 Let $\bar{J}(D, \omega) = \sum_{j=1}^{U} \sum_{\phi \in \Phi_j} \lambda_\phi \phi(\omega)$

 Compute $\omega_* = \text{argmin}_\omega \bar{J}(D, \omega)$

 return ω_*

The functional mechanism can be applied to linear regression. The expansion of objective function $J(D, \omega)$ for linear regression only involves monomials in Φ_0, Φ_1, and Φ_2.

$$J(D, \omega) = \sum_{t_i \in D} (y_i - t_i^T \omega)^2$$

$$= \sum_{t_i \in D} (y_i)^2 - \sum_{j=1}^{d} \left(2 \sum_{t_i \in D} y_i t_{ij} \right) w_j + \sum_{1 \leq j, l \leq d} \left(\sum_{t_i \in D} t_{ij} t_{il} \right) w_j w_l.$$

And the scale of Laplace noise can be bounded by,

$$\Delta = 2 \max_t \sum_{j=1}^{U} \sum_{\phi \in \Phi_j} \|\lambda_{\phi t}\|_1$$

$$\leq 2(1 + 2d + d^2).$$

Note that this sensitivity becomes very large as d increases. Adding noises of this magnitude to every coefficient, and then optimizing for that objective function results in poor performances.

For other regression tasks, e.g., logistic regression, where the objective function is not a polynomial with finite order, Zhang et al. [2012] proposed to use the first two order terms of Taylor expansion to approximate this kind of objective function.

The functional mechanism adds more perturbation to the objective function than the previous method, and thus performs even worse.

5.3   MAKE AN EXISTING ALGORITHM PRIVATE

Another approach is to take a non-private optimization algorithm, and to apply the Laplace mechanism or the exponential mechanism to ensure that every step is private. Oftentimes, one takes an iterative algorithm for an optimization task, and then makes each iteration private. Here, one main parameter is the number of iterations. When the number is too small, then the algorithm is far from converging. On the other hand, when the number is too large, each iteration has very little privacy budget, and too much noise is added to each iteration. Intuitively, this method is sub-optimal because the amount of perturbation added in this approach ensures that outputting all the intermediate results together is private, whereas only the final output is needed.

5.3.1 DPLLOYD: DIFFERENTIALLY PRIVATE LLOYD ALGORITHM FOR k-MEANS CLUSTERING

The k-means clustering problem has been used as a motivating application for PINQ [McSherry, 2009], a platform for interactive privacy preserving data analysis. McSherry implemented k-means clustering using the PINQ system [McSherry]. We call this the DPLloyd approach. DPLloyd fixes the total number of iterations to be 5 in McSherry [2009]. It adds Laplacian noise to the iterative update step in the Lloyd algorithm. Each iteration requires computing the total number of points in a cluster and, for each dimension, the sum of the coordinates of the data points in a cluster. Let d be the number of dimensions. Then, each tuple is involved in answering dt sum queries and t count queries. To bound the sensitivity of the sum query to a small number r, each dimension is normalized to $[-r, r]$. Thus, the global sensitivity of DPLloyd is $(dr + 1)t$ [Dwork et al., 2006], and each query is answered by adding Laplacian noise $\mathsf{Lap}\left(\frac{(dr+1)t}{\epsilon}\right)$.

Algorithm 5.2 DPLloyd

Input: D: dataset, ϵ: privacy parameter, d: number of dimensions, k: number of clusters, t: number of iterations, r: data range $[-r, r]$

  Randomly select k points $o^1, o^2, \ldots, o^k$ as initial centroids
  $e = \frac{\epsilon}{(dr+1)t}$
  for Loop t times **do**
    for each cluster j $(j = 1, 2, \ldots, k)$ **do**
      $C^j = \{x^\ell : \|x^\ell - o^i\| \leq \|x^\ell - o^j\| \forall 1 \leq i \leq k\}$
      $count = |C^j| + \mathsf{Lap}\left(\frac{1}{e}\right)$
      for each dimension i $(i = 1, 2, \ldots, d)$ **do**
        $sum = \sum_{x^\ell \in C^j} x_i^\ell + \mathsf{Lap}\left(\frac{1}{e}\right)$
        $o_i^j = \frac{sum}{count}$
      end for
    end for
  end for
  Return $o^1, o^2, \ldots, o^k$

The algorithm is given in Algorithm 5.2. The overall structure of DPLloyd is to first select initial values, and then iteratively improve them. This same algorithmic structure also applies to many other data analysis tasks, such as linear regression, SVM, etc. When making such an interactive and iterative algorithm differentially private, there are several important decisions one has to make.

The first decision is how to select the initial values. In the standard, non-private setting, a purely random choice may suffice, since one could repeat the algorithm multiple times and choose the best result among them. With privacy constraints, however, running the interactive algorithm multiple times means that each run can use only a fraction of the total privacy budget, causing the results to be less accurate. Thus the choice of initial values becomes more important. In the case of k-means clustering, many methods for choosing the initial points have been developed; see, e.g., Peña et al. [1999]. However, these methods all need access to the dataset, and it is unclear how to perform them in a differentially privately way. Therefore, DPLloyd randomly generates k points as the initial centroids.

The second decision is how many iterations one runs. A large number of iterations causes too much noise to be added. A small number of iterations may be insufficient for the algorithm to converge. Existing approaches fix a number. However, intuitively the number of rounds would depend both on the available privacy budget ϵ and the quality of the initial values. With a smaller privacy budget, one should run fewer numbers of rounds, to avoid the results being overwhelmed by too much noise.

The third decision is how to allocate the privacy budget across different rounds. Almost by default existing approaches allocate privacy budget equally across different rounds. However, intuitively this is not optimal. In later rounds, when one gets closer to the optimal value, it is desirable to have a larger privacy budget.

In the implementation of DPLloyd in PINQ, it is proposed to run five iterations, with equal privacy budget allocation for each round. It appears that this setting works quite well across many datasets. In Mohan et al. [2012], when a method newly proposed for k-means clustering was compared with DPLloyd, the experiments were done by running DPLloyd with 20, 80, and 200 iterations, resulting in artificially poor performance of DPLloyd.

In Dwork [2011], it is proposed that when the number of rounds is not fixed, one uses exponentially decreasing allocation of privacy budgets, i.e., $\frac{\epsilon}{2}$ in the first round, $\frac{\epsilon}{4}$ in the second round, and so on. This mostly likely results in deteriorating performance when the number of rounds increases. Using this method, in later rounds, when one hopes to get closer to the optimal value, increasingly larger noises are added due to the exponentially decreasing privacy budget. If one does not allocate privacy budgets equally across all rounds, then one should allocate smaller privacy budgets for the earlier rounds and larger privacy budgets for the later rounds, although one cannot do that without fixing the total number of rounds.

5.3.2 DIFFPID3: DIFFERENTIAL PRIVATE ID3 ALGORITHM FOR DECISION TREE CLASSIFICATION

In Blum et al. [2005], the algorithm for constructing an ID3 decision tree classifier is made differentially private. When the ID3 algorithm needs to get the number of tuples with a specific feature value, it queries the SuLQ interface to get the corresponding noise count. The DiffPID3 algorithm in Friedman and Schuster [2010] improved this approach by redesigning the classic ID3 classifier construction algorithm to consider the feature quality function with lower sensitivity and using the exponential mechanism to evaluate all the attributes simultaneously. Specifically, the DiffPID3 algorithm starts with the most general partition of the underlying dataset. Then, the algorithm chooses the attribute that maximizes the purity by using the exponential mechanism and splits the dataset with the selected attribute. The same process is applied recursively on each subset of the dataset until there are no further splits that improve the purity.

Algorithm 5.3 DiffPID3

INPUT: D: Dataset, $\mathcal{A} = \{A_1, \ldots, A_d\}$: set of attributes, C: class attribute, ϵ: privacy parameter, d: maximal tree depth, $\epsilon' = \frac{\epsilon}{2(d+1)}$: privacy parameter for each recursive invocation

> $t \leftarrow \max_{A \in \mathcal{A}} |A|$
> $N_D \leftarrow \text{NoisyCount}_{\epsilon'}(D)$
> **if** $\mathcal{A} = \emptyset$ or $d = 0$ or $\frac{N_D}{t|C|} < \frac{\sqrt{2}}{\epsilon'}$ **then**
> > $D_c \leftarrow \text{Partition}(D, \forall c \in C : r_C = c)$
> > $\forall c \in C : N_c = \text{NoisyCount}_{\epsilon'}(D_c)$
> > **return** a leaf labeled with $\text{argmax}_c(N_c)$
> **end if**
> $\bar{A} \leftarrow \text{ExpMech}_{\epsilon'}(\mathcal{A}, q)$
> $D_i \leftarrow \text{Partition}(D, \forall i \in \bar{A} : r_{\bar{A}} = i)$
> **for** each $i \in \bar{A}$ **do**
> > $\text{Subtree}_i \leftarrow \text{DiffPID3}(D_i, \mathcal{A} \setminus \bar{A}, C, d - 1, \epsilon')$
> **end for**
> **return** a tree with a root node labeled $\bar{A}$ and edges labeled 1 to $|\bar{A}|$ each going to subtree$_i$.

5.4   ITERATIVE LOCAL SEARCH VIA EM

Instead of adding making individual steps in an optimization algorithm private, another approach is to iteratively apply the exponential mechanism to gradually improve the current choice of ω. In order to do this, one has to generate a candidate set, e.g., by generating multiple perturbations of the current ω, and then select among the set in a private fashion. We now look at some examples of such algorithms.

5.4.1 PRIVGENE: DIFFERENTIALLY PRIVATE MODEL FITTING USING GENETIC ALGORITHMS

PrivGene [Zhang et al., 2013] is a general-purpose differentially private model fitting framework based on genetic algorithms. Given a dataset D and a fitting function $f(D, \omega)$ that measures how well the parameter ω fits the dataset D, the PrivGene algorithm initializes a candidate set of possible parameters ω and iteratively refines them by mimicking the process of natural evolution. Specifically, in each iteration, PrivGene selects m' parameters from the candidate set, and generates from them offsprings by crossover and mutation. Then, it creates a new parameter set, which includes all and only the offsprings. At the end of the last iteration, a single parameter is selected and outputted as the final result.

Algorithm 5.4 PrivGene

INPUT D: Dataset, J: objective function, ϵ: privacy parameter, m, m' :sizes of candidate set Ω and selected set Ω', r: number of iterations

Output ω: best parameter vector identified by PrivGene

   Initialize candidate set Ω with m randomly generated vectors

   for $i = 1$ to $r - 1$ **do**

      $\Omega' \leftarrow \text{DPSelect}(D, J, \Omega, m', \epsilon/r)$

      $\Omega \leftarrow \{\}$

      for $j = 1$ to $m/2$ **do**

         Randomly choose two vectors $\omega^1, \omega^2 \in \Omega'$ as parent parameters

         Compute $(v^1, v^2) \leftarrow \text{Crossover}(\omega^1, \omega^2)$

         Mutate(v^1) and Mutate(v^2)

         Add two offspring parameters v^1, v^2 to Ω

      end for

   end for

   $\{\omega\} \leftarrow \text{DPSelect}(D, J, \Omega, 1, \epsilon/r)$

   return ω

This algorithm is given in Algorithm 5.4. PrivGene is applied to logistic regression, SVM, and k-means clustering. In the case of k-means clustering, the NICV formula in Equation 5.1, more precisely its non-normalized version, is used as the fitting function f, and the set of k cluster centroids is defined as parameter ω. Initially, the candidate set is populated with 200 sets of cluster centroids randomly sampled from the data space, each set containing exactly k centroids. Then, the algorithm runs iteratively for $N\epsilon/(800m')$ rounds, where m' is empirically set to 10, and N is the dataset size.

While the idea of making a genetic programming algorithm differentially private is interesting, the effectiveness of Algorithm 5.4 is questionable for several reasons. First, the crossover operation often does not result in competitive candidates. Second, with crossover and mutation,

Algorithm 5.5 DPSelect

INPUT D: Dataset, J: objective function, Ω: parameter candidate set, m': number of parameter vectors to be selected from Ω, ϵ_s: privacy parameter

Output Ω': set of selected parameter vectors

  $\Omega' \leftarrow \{\}$

  For each $\omega \in \Omega$, compute $J(D, \omega)$

  for $i = 1$ to m' **do**

    Use privacy budget ϵ_s / m' to apply the exponential mechanism to select the parameter vector ω_* from Ω that aims to minimize $J(D, \omega_*)$.

    Remove ω_* from Ω, and add ω_* to Ω'

  end for

  return Ω_l

the convergence rate is low, which means a larger number of iterations is needed. Third, for each iteration, the algorithm requires making m' selections, with every single one of them consuming some privacy budget.

5.4.2   ITERATIVE LOCAL SEARCH

A more effective local search algorithm can be developed using some ideas from the PrivGene paper, but does not use features of genetic programming. Such an algorithm is implemented in the code accompanying the PrivGene paper [Zhang et al., 2013], even though the algorithm did not appear in the paper. We give the algorithm below.

This algorithm has several interesting ideas. Each round, it uses the exponential mechanism to select a single local perturbation that improves the current solution the best. Compared with PrivGene, which selects multiple candidates (for the purpose of using crossovers to generate the pool of candidates), this means that more privacy budgets can be used in each selection. Since only one candidate is selected, there is no crossover. The mutation step takes the form of perturbing the coefficient in one dimension. That is, each iteration can be viewed as moving along one dimension toward a potentially better parameter. Finally, the perturbation step s exponentially decays so that the amount of changes decreases. This makes sense as when one starts to converge to the optimal parameter, smaller adjustments are needed. Also, this feature of exponential decay of the perturbation step can also take advantage of the enhanced exponential mechanism, to be discussed below. This method is most useful when the goal is to find a vector of coefficients, as in the case of logistic regression and SVM.

5.4.3   ENHANCED EXPONENTIAL MECHANISM

An enhanced version of the exponential mechanism (EEM) is proposed in Zhang et al. [2013], which can be used in the iterative local search algorithm. Recall that the quality function we

Algorithm 5.6 ExpSearch

INPUT D: Dataset, J: objective function, ϵ: privacy parameter, r: number of iterations, ω_0: initial parameter, s: step of search, $\beta < 1$: scaling parameter
Output ω: selected parameter

$\omega \leftarrow \omega_0$
for $i = 1$ to $r - 1$ **do**
   $\Omega \leftarrow \{\}$
   for $j \in \{1..d\}$ **do**
      $\omega_1 \leftarrow \omega$ with j's attribute $+ s$
      $\omega_2 \leftarrow \omega$ with j's attribute $- s$
      $\Omega \leftarrow \Omega \cup \{\omega_1, \omega_2\}$
      compute $J(D, \omega_1)$ and $J(D, \omega_2)$
   end for
   $\omega \leftarrow$ Use privacy budget ϵ/r to apply the exponential mechanism to select the parameter vector ω_* from Ω that aims to maximize $J(D, \omega_*)$.
   $s \leftarrow s * \beta$
end for
return ω

use is the optimization objective function $J(D, \omega)$. In the standard exponential mechanism, one considers the maximal difference between the values of the quality function on two neighboring datasets D and D', i.e., $\Delta J = \max_{\forall \omega, D \simeq D'} |J(D, \omega) - J(D', \omega)|$.

EEM is suitable for the case where the dependency of the quality function on the dataset D can be computed by summing up some score for each record $t \in D$, i.e.,

$$J(D, \omega) = c(\omega) + \sum_{x \in D} L_\omega(x).$$

In this case, when making a selection among a set Ω, one could also use as global sensitivity the maximal difference between $L_\omega(x)$ and $L_{\omega'}(x)$ where $\omega, \omega' \in \Omega$, and x is any data element in the input dataset. This is particularly effective in the local search paradigm where the set of candidates are all minor perturbations, and thus $\max_{x, \omega, \omega'} (|L_\omega(x) - L_{\omega'}(x)|)$ may be small.

In EEM, one selects $\omega \in \Omega$ with probability proportional to $e^{\epsilon J(D, \omega)/(2\Delta_J)}$, where

$$\Delta = \min \left\{ \Delta_1 = \max_{x, x' \in D, \omega \in \Omega} \left| L_\omega(x) - L_\omega(x') \right|, \Delta_2 = \max_{x \in D, \omega, \omega' \in \Omega} \left| L_\omega(x) - L_{\omega'}(x) \right| \right\}.$$

Δ_1 is exactly the global sensitivity used in the standard exponential mechanism (here the bounded interpretation of DP is used), while Δ_2 is a new global sensitivity designed specifically for additive quality functions.

When EEM is used in PrivGene and iterative local search, Δ_2 is usually smaller than Δ_1. This is because as more iterations are performed, it is likely that the maximum value of $L_\omega(x) - L_{\omega'}(x)$ gradually decreases with the number of iterations performed, leading to decreasing Δ_2. Δ_1, on the other hand, is not significantly affected by this phenomenon. Therefore, EEM can make a more accurate selection in each iteration as the algorithm converges.

5.5   HISTOGRAMS OPTIMIZED FOR OPTIMIZATION

The final approach we consider is to publish a synopsis of the dataset, often in the form of a noisy histogram, so that synthetic datasets can be generated and optimizers can be learned from these synthetic datasets. Publishing a synopsis enables additional exploratory and predictive data analysis tasks to be performed, and can be argued to be preferred.

5.5.1   UNIFORM GRID AND ITS EXTENSIONS

For low-dimensional datasets with numerical attributes, UG and its extension can be applied. UG (Uniform Grid) is a simple algorithm proposed in Qardaji et al. [2013c] for producing synopsis of two-dimensional datasets that can be used to answer rectangular range queries (i.e., how many data points there are in a rectangular range) with high accuracy. The algorithm partitions the space into $M = m \times m$ equal-width grid cells, and then releases the noisy count in each cell. It is observed that for counting queries, a larger M value results in higher errors because more noises are added, and a smaller M value results in higher errors due to the fact that points within cells may be distributed nonuniformly, and queries including a portion of these cells may be answered inaccurately. To balance these two kinds of errors, it is suggested to set

$$m = \sqrt{\frac{N\epsilon}{10}}, \text{ or equivalently, } M = \frac{N\epsilon}{10}. \tag{5.4}$$

It has been shown that UG performs quite well for answering rectangular range queries [Qardaji et al., 2013c].

In Su et al. [2016b], UG is extended to a higher-dimensional case by setting

$$M = \left(\frac{N\epsilon}{\theta}\right)^{\frac{2d}{2+d}}, \tag{5.5}$$

where $\theta = 10$. And the new algorithm is called extended uniform grid, EUG. When the dimensionality d increases, this approach does not scale very well.

5.5.2   HISTOGRAM PUBLISHING FOR ESTIMATING M-ESTIMATORS

Lei [2011] proposed a scheme to release a differentially private histogram tailored for the M-estimator. Similar to UG and EUG, it partitions the data space into equal-width grid cells. However, it uses a different method to determine how many grid cells to use. Given a d-dimensional dataset with N tuples, statistical analysis in Lei [2011] suggests that

$$M = \left(\frac{N}{\sqrt{\log(N)}} \right)^{\frac{2d}{2+d}}. \tag{5.6}$$

Theoretical bounds on accuracy for M-estimator are a generalization of maximum likelihood estimation. Given a dataset $D = \{x^1, x^2, \ldots, x^N\}$ and a target function ρ, it determines a parameter ω_*, such that

$$\omega_* = \underset{\boldsymbol{\omega}}{\text{argmin}} \sum_{\ell=1}^{N} \rho(x^\ell, \omega).$$

Note that the only difference between the above approach and UG is in how the number of cells is determined. We note that unlike UG, the above approach for choosing M does not depend on ϵ.

5.5.3 DIFFGEN: DIFFERENTIALLY PRIVATE ANONYMIZATION BASED ON GENERALIZATION

Mohammed et al. [2011] proposed DiffGen to publish a histogram for classification under differential privacy. It consists of two steps: partition and perturbation. Given a dataset D and taxonomy trees for each predictor attribute, the partition step starts by generalizing all attributes' values into the topmost nodes in their taxonomy trees and then iteratively selects one attribute's taxonomy tree node at a time for specialization by using the standard exponential mechanism. The quality of each candidate specialization is based on the same heuristics used by the decision tree constructions, such as information gain and majority class. The partition step terminates after a given number of specializations. The perturbation step injects Laplace noise into each cell of the partition and outputs all the cells with their noisy counts as the noisy synopsis of the data. The privacy budget needs to be evenly distributed to all the levels in the tree. Thus, only a small portion of budget can be assigned to each node splitting. This would result in the histogram being structured to be far from optimal and result in poor performance of the algorithm.

5.5.4 PRIVPFC: DIFFERENTIALLY PRIVATE DATA PUBLICATION FOR CLASSIFICATION

PrivPfC is an algorithm proposed in Su et al. [2016a] for producing a synopsis for multi-attribute datasets with high classification accuracy. For a multi-attribute dataset with more than a dozen or so attributes, publishing a histogram with all the attributes results in a sparse histogram where noises may overwhelm the true counts. Therefore it is necessary to select a subset of the attributes that are "useful" for the intended data analysis tasks, and to determine how to discretize the attributes. These selections partition the domain into a number of cells. We call the result a "grid."

On the key decision of how to select a grid, PrivPfC differs from previous approaches in that it selects a high-quality grid in a single step, whereas previous approaches use an iterative process and as a consequence suffer from two weaknesses. First, an iterative process has to divide the privacy budget among all the iterations, causing the choice made in each iteration to have significant noise. Second, an iterative process is a greedy process and tends to result in a sub-optimal global choice even without considering noises.

PrivPfC has two novel ideas. One is a method to enumerate through candidate grids when given a cap on how many grids the algorithm is allowed to consider; and the other is a new quality function that enables the selection of a high-quality "grid." This quality function considers the impact of injected noises on the classification accuracy, adapts to the privacy parameter ϵ, and has a low sensitivity.

Given the dataset, the privacy budget and the maximum grid pool size, PrivPfC first enumerates all possible grids, which partitions the data domain into a number of cells, in a level-wise approach and puts them into a pool with given size. Then, it privately selects a high-quality grid in a single step, by using the exponential mechanism with a novel quality function, which maximizes the expected number of correctly classified records by a histogram classifier. Finally, PrivPfC injects noises into each cell of the selected grid and releases the noisy grid as the private synopsis of the data.

Both PrivPfC and DiffGen publish noisy histogram for classifications. The key difference between PrivPfC and DiffGen is that PrivPfC determines the histogram structure, the grid g, in a single step, instead of iteratively choosing the attributes and ways to partition the data space. There are two reasons why such an iterative approach does not perform well. The first is that the decisions made in each iteration may be sub-optimal because of the randomization necessary for satisfying differential privacy. The second is that even if the decision made in each iteration is locally optimal, the combination of them is not globally optimal.

5.6   BIBLIOGRAPHICAL NOTES

See Su et al. [2016b] for a detailed comparison of different algorithms on k-means clustering; the currently known best performing algorithms are DPLloyd and EUGkM. The performances of other algorithms are much worse.

See Su et al. [2016a] for a detailed comparison of different algorithms on classification algorithms. For the goal of constructing classification trees, PrivPfC performs the best. For the goals of logistic regression and SVM, PrivPfC and private local search, which are variants of PrivGene [Zhang et al., 2013], perform the best.

Algorithm 5.7 PrivPfC: Differentially Privately Publishing Data for Classification

---

Input: dataset D, the set of predictor variables A and their taxonomy hierarchies, total privacy budget ϵ, maximum grid pool size Ω.

$\epsilon_N \leftarrow 0.03\epsilon, \epsilon_{sh} \leftarrow 0.37\epsilon, \epsilon_{ph} \leftarrow 0.6\epsilon$
$\hat{N} \leftarrow |D| + \mathrm{Lap}(1/\epsilon_N)$
$T \leftarrow 20\% \cdot \hat{N} \cdot \epsilon_{ph}$
$\mathsf{H} \leftarrow \mathrm{Enumerate}(\mathsf{A}, \Omega, T)$
Comment: privately select grid
for $i = 1 \rightarrow |\mathsf{H}|$ **do**
    $q_i \leftarrow \mathrm{qual}(\mathsf{H}_i)$
    $p_i \leftarrow e^{-(q_i \epsilon_{sh})/2}$
end for
$h \leftarrow$ sample $i \in [1..|\mathsf{H}|]$ according to p_i
Initialize I to empty   Comment: privately perturb grid
for each cell $c \in h$ **do**
    $\hat{n}_c^+ \leftarrow n_c^+ + \mathrm{Lap}(1/\epsilon_{ph})$
    $\hat{n}_c^- \leftarrow n_c^- + \mathrm{Lap}(1/\epsilon_{ph})$
    Add $(\hat{n}_c^+, \hat{n}_c^-)$ to I
end for
Round all counts of I to their nearest non-negative integers.
return $\hat{I}$

CHAPTER 6

Publishing Marginals

In this chapter we consider the problem of computing a differentially private synopsis of a high-dimensional dataset so that one can reconstruct any low-dimensional marginal tables of the dataset. Marginal tables are the workhorses of categorical data analysis, e.g., data analysis in the medical, social, and behavior sciences. In addition to being easy to interpret, they are sufficient statistics for popular classes of probabilistic models. Because of this, they are the methods of choice for government agencies when releasing statistical summaries of categorical data. Marginal tables are essentially equivalent to OLAP (online analytical processing) cubes used in data management and analysis. Marginal tables can be constructed directly by counting queries, which has been the center of focus for differentially private data analysis.

6.1 PROBLEM DEFINITION

Following the literature, we limit ourselves to binary datasets. We consider the following problem: given a d-dimensional binary dataset D, and a positive integer $k < d$, we want to differentially privately construct a synopsis of D, so that any k-way *marginal contingency table* (marginal table for short) can be computed with reasonable accuracy.

We now elaborate on this problem definition. D is a dataset that has d binary attributes; thus the set of all attributes can be defined as $\mathbf{A} = \{1, 2, \cdots, d\}$. Each tuple t in D is a binary string in $\{0, 1\}^d$.

Information in D can be equivalently represented using the full contingency table, which has 2^d entries, one for each string $\{0, 1\}^d$. Each entry gives the number of times the corresponding string occurs in D. When one wants to analyze the relationships among some of the attributes in $\mathbf{A}$, marginal tables can be constructed, by summing corresponding entries in the contingency table. More specifically, for any subset $A \subseteq \mathbf{A}$ of $k = |A|$ attributes, the marginal table for A has 2^k entries, one corresponding to each possible assignment of the k attributes in A. We call a marginal table for a set of k attributes a k-way marginal table.

Utility Goal. The utility goal is to generate k-way marginals that are close to the true values. Since we do not know which attributes are likely to be of interest, every k-way marginal is likely to be of interest. We thus assume that the goal is to be able to answer every k-way marginal query. Given a generated k-way marginal table $\tilde{\mathsf{T}}_A$ for a set A of attributes, we consider two error measures and aim at minimizing them.

The first is the L_2 distance between $\tilde{\mathsf{T}}_A$ and T_A, the k-way marginal table over A computed from the original dataset, when both are viewed as vectors consisting of 2^k elements. We call this the **error distance**. For a given method, the error distance is a random variable as its value depends on the noise added by the method. The expected value of the square of error distance is also the expected value of the sum of squared errors in each cell, and we call it the **Expected Squared Error (ESE)**. We often use the ESE to understand a method's utility.

The second is the Jensen-Shannon divergence between $\mathsf{norm}(\tilde{\mathsf{T}}_A)$ and $\mathsf{norm}(\mathsf{T}_A)$, where norm normalizes a marginal table by dividing each cell with the sum of all the cells, so that in the normalized table the sum of all cells equals 1. It is natural to use the Kullback-Leibler divergence between $\mathsf{norm}(\mathsf{T}_A)$ and $\mathsf{norm}(\tilde{\mathsf{T}}_A)$, since $D_{\mathsf{KL}}(P||Q)$ measures the information lost when Q is used to approximate P. However, $D_{\mathsf{KL}}(P||Q)$ is undefined when $Q(i) = 0$ and $P(i) \neq 0$ for some i, which can happen in our setting. We thus choose to use Jensen-Shannon divergence [Lin, 1991], which is a symmetrized and smoothed version of the Kullback-Leibler divergence:

$$D_{\mathsf{JS}}(P||Q) = \frac{1}{2}D_{KL}(P||M) + \frac{1}{2}D_{KL}(Q||M), \tag{6.1}$$

where $M = \frac{P+Q}{2}$ and $D_{\mathsf{KL}(P||Q)} = \sum_i \ln\left(\frac{P(i)}{Q(i)}\right) P(i)$.

Efficiency requirement. Let $N = |D|$ denote the number of tuples in the dataset. We assume that $N \ll 2^d$, and thus want to avoid $\Theta(2^d)$ computational complexity. We assume that k is relatively small compared with d, that is, running time in the low-degree polynomial in 2^k is acceptable. Note that a k-way marginal has 2^k entries, thus the complexity linear in 2^k is unavoidable.

6.2   METHODS THAT DON'T FIT THE PROBLEM

We first describe several methods that do not work well for the settings we consider.

6.2.1   THE FLAT METHOD

A basic approach, henceforth referred to as the Flat method, is to generate a noisy version of the full contingency table of D. In this method, one adds noise from distribution $\mathsf{Lap}\left(\frac{1}{\epsilon}\right)$ to all counts in the full contingency table of the dataset. This noisy full contingency table can then be used to compute any k-way marginal tables. This approach takes time $O(2^d)$.

To estimate the ESE, we observe that the noise added to each cell of the full contingency table has variance

$$V_u = \frac{2}{\epsilon^2}. \tag{6.2}$$

We treat V_u as the unit of ESE. To reconstruct a k-way marginal table, one sums up the noisy counts for the corresponding cells in the contingency table. For each entry in the k-way marginal table, one sums up 2^{d-k} cells, and the marginal table has 2^k entries, each with independently generated noise. Thus, the ESE of the Flat method is

$$2^k \times 2^{d-k} V_u = 2^d V_u. \tag{6.3}$$

This approach works very well when d is small. An analysis of its accuracy was provided in Lei [2011]. However, when d is large it suffers from two problems. First, the time complexity and space complexity are both $\Theta(2^d)$, which is too large for larger values of d. Second, it will be highly inaccurate, as the ESE increases exponentially in d.

6.2.2 THE DIRECT METHOD

Another method is to add independently generated Laplacian noise to each k-way marginal table. The method was used in Dwork et al. [2006]. To compute m marginal tables while satisfying ϵ-DP, one adds noise sampled from $\mathsf{Lap}\left(\frac{m}{\epsilon}\right)$ to each entry, resulting in a variance of $m^2 V_u$. As $m = \binom{d}{k}$ and each table has 2^k entries, this results in an ESE of

$$2^k \binom{d}{k}^2 V_u. \tag{6.4}$$

Comparing Equations (6.4) and (6.3), we can see that for smaller values of d, the Flat method is better. The Direct method starts outperforming the Flat method for larger d's. The exact values of d's for which the Direct method overtakes the Flat method depend on k and are given in the table below.

k	2	3	4	5
Condition for Direct better than Flat	$d \geq 16$	$d \geq 26$	$d \geq 36$	$d \geq 46$

Equations (6.3) and (6.4) may over-estimate the error, especially when the computed value is greater than 1. This is because large noises may result in negative values, which can be corrected. However, this over-estimation becomes significant only when there are large negative values, in which case the error will remain large even after correcting them. For example, suppose that one noise entry is close to $-\frac{N}{2}$; then this means that the noise added to each entry is likely large enough to overwhelm the true counts in most cells.

The direct method has time complexity $\Theta(\max(d^k, N))$ and space complexity of $\Theta(d^k)$; while the flat method has time and space complexity of $\Theta(\max(2^d, N))$. When k is small, the direct method scales much better than the flat method when d increases.

6.2.3 ADDING NOISE IN THE FOURIER DOMAIN

Barak et al. [2007] proposed the approach to add noises in the Fourier domain. Conceptually, each full contingency table corresponds to a set of 2^d Fourier coefficients, and each k-way marginal can be reconstructed using 2^k of these coefficients. To reconstruct all k-way marginals, one needs $1 + \binom{d}{1} + \binom{d}{2} + \cdots + \binom{d}{k}$ coefficients (corresponding to all binary strings with at most k 1's). One can publish noisy versions of these coefficients, which can be subsequently used to reconstruct any desired k-way marginal. The magnitude of noise added to the coefficients is similar to that in the direct method.

One potential advantage of this approach over the Direct method is that because there is a one-to-one correspondence between full contingency tables and the vectors of Fourier coefficients, the noisy marginals reconstructed from noisy Fourier coefficients are consistent in the sense that there exists a full contingency table that corresponds to the generated noisy marginals. However, the corresponding marginal table may contain negative entries. To avoid such negative entries, it is proposed to use linear programming to compute a full contingency table that does not contain any negative entries, while minimizing the largest error between the noisy Fourier coefficients and the Fourier coefficients computed from the contingency table.

Using linear programming to compute a full contingency table, which has 2^d entries, is unfeasible when d is large. When the linear programming step is not used, the method becomes adding noise to the Fourier coefficients, and then reconstructing the k-way marginal. This has similar accuracy as the Direct method.

6.2.4 DATA CUBES

Ding et al. [2011] tries to solve the following problem. Given a set of attributes, which marginals should one publish if the goal is to answer a set of marginal queries as accurately as possible? The main idea is illustrated by the following example. For example, if the goal is to compute marginals for each of two attributes, the best choice depends on how many values each of these attributes have. When each of these attributes has very few values (such as the case of binary attributes), the optimal approach is to publish one marginal for the pair of attributes. When each of these attributes has many values, then it is better to split the privacy budget and publish two marginals, one for each attribute. In the case of binary attributes, the principles in Ding et al. [2011] will lead it to choose to publish the full contingency table, which is equivalent to the Flat method.

Another limitation of the approach in Ding et al. [2011] is that the techniques, both for view selection and for view consistency, require traversal of the lattice of all subsets of the attributes. In our problem setting, this requires time polynomial in 2^d, and is thus unfeasible in our setting. This approach first organizes all possible marginals in a lattice under the subset relation. With a d-dimensional binary dataset, there are 2^d marginals in the lattice. The approach then iteratively selects which marginals should be released. In each iteration, it traverses all 2^d marginals in the lattice and greedily selects one. The consistency technique is also polynomial in 2^d because it constructs all marginals in the lattice that are above the chosen ones in order to achieve consistency.

6.2.5 MULTIPLICATIVE WEIGHTS MECHANISM

Several approaches based on multiplicative updates were proposed in Gupta et al. [2011], Hardt and Rothblum [2010], Hardt et al. [2012]. In these approaches, one maintains and improves a distribution approximating a given dataset for answering a set of counting queries. We consider the non-interactive version of the approach by Hardt et al. [2012], which we use MWEM to denote. To release k-way marginals, the approach works as follows. The set of queries is the set of all k-way marginals. One starts with an initial full contingency table that is uniform, and then selects, using the exponential mechanism, a k-way marginal that is most incorrectly answered by the current distribution. One then obtains a noisy answer to the selected marginal, and updates the distribution to match the current state of knowledge. This process is repeated T times. Each round is allocated a privacy budget ϵ / T. Half of the privacy budget at each round is used to select a marginal that is most incorrectly answered, and the other half is used to get a noisy answer. The basic version of MWEM performs a single multiplicative update step in each round using the new query, and outputs the average from the distribution after each round. A theorem provides a utility bound for this method.

Experiments in Hardt et al. [2012] use the following two improvements over the basic version. In each round, one iterates over all existing query results 100 times to attempt to maximally benefit from the query results. Furthermore, queries are answered using the final distribution instead of using the average. While these improvements greatly improved the actual performance in practice, using them means that the theoretically proven utility bound no longer holds.

Maintaining a full contingency table requires time and space complexity $\Omega(2^d)$, and is unfeasible for larger d values. The largest d value used in Hardt et al. [2012] is $d = 16$. A technique is introduced in Hardt et al. [2012] to avoid explicitly storing the full contingency table. This technique, however, is limited to the case when the attributes can be partitioned into disjoint parts so that no query involves attributes from more than one part, which is not applicable to our problem.

6.2.6 LEARNING BASED APPROACHES

Another line of work on private releasing of marginal tables uses an interesting perspective introduced in Gupta et al. [2011]. Instead of viewing a set of queries as a set of functions on the database, this approach views a database as a function on queries. More specifically, given the set of N counting queries that one wants to be answered, let $\ell = \lceil \log_2 N \rceil$; we can index these queries using a binary string in $\{0, 1\}^\ell$. Then the database D can be viewed as a function $f_D : \{0, 1\}^\ell \to [0, 1]$, mapping each query to a fraction between 0 and 1, which gives the fraction of tuples in D that satisfies the query. The goal is thus to learn a good approximation of f_D while satisfying differential privacy.

A number of papers followed up this approach [Cheraghchi et al., 2012, Dwork et al., 2010, Gupta et al., 2012a, Thaler et al., 2012]. The state-of-the-art approach in this line of work, which is also the most practical, is Thaler et al. [2012]. The high-level idea is as follows: to approximate the function f_D, observe that each tuple t in D can be viewed as a predicate $f_t : \{0, 1\}^\ell \to \{0, 1\}$. For any query q indexed by a string in $\{0, 1\}^\ell$, if the tuple t satisfies the query q and should be counted, then $f_t(q) = 1$; otherwise, $f_t(q) = 0$. To approximate $f_t : \{0, 1\}^\ell \to \{0, 1\}$, we view it as a function of ℓ binary variables $(y_1, y_2, \cdots, y_\ell)$ (instead of as a function of one variable taking 2^ℓ values), and approximate it using a multi-variate real-coefficients polynomial $g_t(y_1, y_2, \cdots, y_\ell)$.

The algorithm in Thaler et al. [2012] works as follows. First, for each tuple $t \in D$, compute a γ-accurate polynomial g_t using the Chebyshev polynomials. Such an approximation is able to approximate f_t to within an error bound γ, that is,

$$\forall q \; [\;\; ((f_t(q) = 0) \Rightarrow (g_t(q) = 0))$$
$$\wedge \; (f_t(q) = 1) \Rightarrow (1 - \gamma \le f_t(q) - g_t(q) \le 1 + \gamma)] .$$

Then compute $g_D(q)$ using the following equation:

$$g_D(y_1, y_2, \cdots, y_\ell) = \frac{\sum_{t \in D} g_t(y_1, y_2, \cdots, y_\ell)}{|D|}. \tag{6.5}$$

Then add Laplacian noise to all the coefficients to $g_D(y_1, y_2, \cdots, y_\ell)$, and publish the noisy polynomial. This serves as a differentially private approximation of $f_D(q)$. Finally, one can compute each entry of the marginal tables by evaluating the noisy polynomial on the query corresponding to the entry. This approach has two sources of errors: approximation error due to using g_D to approximate f_D and noise error due to adding Laplacian noises to coefficients of g_D.

An important parameter that greatly affects both the running time and accuracy of this method is P, the number of terms in polynomials g_D. Noise linear in P is added to each coefficient. P is determined by ℓ, the number of variables in the polynomial g_t, and p, the degree of the polynomial. More specifically, $P = \binom{\ell+p}{p}$. To construct k-way marginal tables, one needs to set $\ell = 2d$. The degree of the polynomial is given by $p = 2\lceil \sqrt{k} \rceil \log(1/\gamma)$, where γ bounds the inaccuracy of using the polynomial g_t to approximate f_t. The following table shows the P values for different combinations of parameters.

		$d = 9, k = 2$			$d = 32, k = 4$	
$\gamma =$	1/2	1/4	1/8	1/2	1/4	1/8
$p =$	4	8	16	4	8	16
$P \approx$	7315	1.56E6	2.2E9	8.1E5	1.2E10	2.6E16

By reducing γ, one reduces the approximation error, but at the same time increases the noise error. We present the numbers for $d = 9$ above because for larger d's, we could not run the implementation for both $\gamma = 1/2$ and $\gamma = 1/4$. Of course, for $d = 9$, the Flat method would work very well. For $d = 32$ and $k = 4$, even setting $\gamma = 1/2$, in which case the approximation may be very inaccurate (a tuple that should be counted as 1 would be counted with a number between 1/2 and 3/2) will result in very large amount of noise added. Setting $\gamma = 1/4$ leads to $P \approx 1.2 \times 10^{10}$. Not only are the time and space requirements of the algorithm impractical, the amount of noise that needs to be added would also be very large because the sensitivity is proportional to $P \cdot 2^p$. (The estimation of sensitivity in Lemma A.1 of Thaler et al. [2012] is essentially $\ell^{O(p)}$, which appears prohibitively large even for small values of d and k.)

In summary, while the learning-based approach in Thaler et al. [2012] gives asymptotically appealing results, it is impractical for the ranges of parameters that are of practical relevance. The complexity $d^{C\sqrt{k}\log(1/\gamma)}$ is asymptotically better than the $\binom{d}{k}2^k$ complexity of the direct method; however, for smaller k's, this complexity is actually much worse. The complexity bound suggests that when k is between 60 and 100, this method can start outperforming the direct method; however, the method (and, in fact, all methods) will become computationally unfeasible long before k reaches that range, e.g., a k-way marginal requires $\Theta(2^k)$ storage.

6.3   THE PRIVIEW APPROACH

The PriView approach, introduced in Qardaji et al. [2014], developed several techniques that when combined solve the marginal problem reasonably well. One key observation is that in order to compute, e.g., a marginal for attributes $\{a, b, c\}$, it is unnecessary to have a marginal whose attributes form a superset of $\{a, b, c\}$. Suppose we have marginals for $\{a, b\}$, $\{a, c\}$, and $\{b, c\}$, then we can compute a marginal for $\{a, b, c\}$ that is consistent with all three known marginals. Of course, such an approximation is inaccurate when there is correlation among attributes in $\{a, b, c\}$ that is not captured by pair-wise correlations. One example is when $a = b\,\mathsf{XOR}\,c$. However, when there is no such strong and somewhat unnatural correlation, the approximation is likely quite accurate.

From this observation, each dataset can be represented by a number of noisy views; each view is a marginal for some subset of attributes. Here a major challenge is to ensure that these views are consistent, which can be solved by extending the constrained inference techniques discussed in Chapter 4.

Notation. We use T_A to denote the noisy marginal table over $A \subseteq \mathbf{A}$. Let Q_A denote the set of all possible counting queries by assigning each attribute in A a value of either 0 or 1. Then T_A can be viewed as a function $\mathsf{T}_A : Q_A \to \mathcal{R}$, where $\mathcal{R}$ is the set of real numbers. We use $\mathsf{T}_A \equiv \mathsf{T}'_A$ to denote that the two marginal tables over A are the same for every entry. And $\mathsf{T}_A(\cdot) \geq x$ to mean that every entry in the table is greater than x. Given T_A, and $A' \subseteq A$, we use $\mathsf{T}_A[A']$ to denote the marginal over A' constructed from T_A by summing the corresponding entries. In particular, $\mathsf{T}_A[\emptyset]$ gives the sum of all cells in T_A.

Definition 6.1 View Consistency. We say that two marginal tables T_{V_i} and T_{V_j} are **consistent** if and only if the marginal table over attributes in $V_i \cap V_j$ reconstructed from T_{V_i} is exactly the same as that reconstructed from T_{V_j}, that is, $\mathsf{T}_{V_i}[V_i \cap V_j] \equiv \mathsf{T}_{V_j}[V_i \cap V_j]$.

6.3.1   SUMMARY OF THE PRIVIEW APPROACH

We now give a summary of our PriView approach, which has the following steps.

1. **Choose the Set of Views.** The first step is to choose which marginal tables to generate. More specifically, we need to choose the set of views:

$$\mathbf{V} = \{V_1, V_2, \ldots, V_w\},$$

where each view $V_i \subseteq \mathbf{A}$ for $1 \leq i \leq w$ and $\bigcup_{i=1...w} V_i = \mathbf{A}$.

2. **Generate Noisy Views.** In this step, for each view V_i we construct a differentially private marginal table, T_{V_i}, by adding Laplace noise $\mathsf{Lap}\left(\frac{w}{\epsilon}\right)$ to the counts specified by the table. This is the only step in the PriView approach that needs direct access to the dataset D. After this step, the dataset D is no longer accessed.

3. **Consistency Step.** In this step, we perform constrained inference on the marginal tables T_{V_i}'s. This step serves two purposes. First, by exploiting existing redundancy among views, it improves the accuracy of T_{V_i}'s. Second, it ensures that for any $i \neq j$, T_{V_i} and T_{V_j} are consistent. (See Definition 6.1 above.) This enables more accurate computation of marginals not fully covered by any view.

4. **Generating k-way Marginals.** Finally, we propose to use the maximum entropy method to generate an arbitrary k-way marginal table based on the T_{V_i}'s.

In the rest of this section, we present the steps of our PriView approach in the reverse order.

6.3.2   COMPUTING k-WAY MARGINALS

Given a set of marginals produced from views in $\mathbf{V}$ that are mutually consistent, and a set A of attributes, where $|A| = k$, we want to compute the k-way marginal T_A. When all the attributes in A are "covered" by at least one view V_i, i.e., $A \subseteq V_i$, this step is trivial. We can construct T_A by summing over corresponding entries in T_{V_i}. However, when $A \not\subseteq V_i$ for each $V_i \in \mathbf{V}$, we need a method to return the marginal which best represents what we know about it.

Given A, for any view V_i, if $A \cap V_i = \emptyset$, then T_{V_i} provides no information. When $A \cap V_i$ contains j attributes, then T_{V_i} provides 2^j linear constraints on cells for T_A. Constraints obtained from different views, however, may not be linearly independent. Thus, we can extract all linearly independent constraints from all views. Unless A is fully contained in some view, the number of linearly independent constraints will always be less than 2^k. The combination of all constraints from all intersecting views results in an *under-specified* system of equations.

We now describe three approaches that can be used in the reconstruction step.

Linear programming.   One strategy is to adopt the linear programming approach proposed in Barak et al. [2007], that is, to compute a marginal so that all the entries are non-negative, and the constraints are satisfied as much as possible.

$$
\begin{aligned}
\text{minimize} \quad & \tau \\
\text{subject to} \quad & \mathop{\forall}_{a \in Q_A} \mathsf{T}_A(a) \geq 0 \\
& \mathop{\forall}_{V_i \in \mathbf{V}} \mathop{\forall}_{a' \in Q_{V_i \cap A}} \left| \mathsf{T}_{V_i}(a') - \mathsf{T}_A(a') \right| \leq \tau.
\end{aligned}
$$

In the above, τ is the maximum error for all constraints. This approach does not require the marginals for the views to be consistent. This approach is unsatisfying in that it considers consistency with regard to the constraints as the only factor in choosing a solution. Recall that we have under-specified constraints for the marginal table, and when they are consistent there is more than one solution. The linear programming method has *no preference* among the set of consistent solutions. We thus consider other methods below. These methods all assume that all views are consistent.

Least Square Solution. One common approach to solving underdetermined systems of equations is to select the solution that has the least L_2 norm. We can thus express the problem of computing a k-way marginal as the following optimization

$$
\begin{aligned}
\text{minimize} \quad & \sum_{a \in Q_A} \mathsf{T}_A(a)^2 \\
\text{subject to} \quad & \underset{a \in Q_A}{\forall} \; \mathsf{T}_A(a) \geq 0 \\
& \underset{V_i \in \mathbf{V}}{\forall} \; \underset{a' \in Q_{V_i \cap A}}{\forall} \; \mathsf{T}_{V_i}(a') = \mathsf{T}_A(a').
\end{aligned}
$$

One can use standard quadratic programming approaches to solve the above optimization problem.

Maximum Entropy. The problem we have at hand is the estimation of a probability distribution with partial information. A common approach is to apply the Principle of Maximum Entropy. In Bayesian probability theory, the principle of maximum entropy states that, subject to precisely stated prior data (a set of precise constraints), the probability distribution which best represents the current state of knowledge is the one with largest information-theoretical entropy. We can thus express the problem of computing a k-way marginal as the following optimization

$$
\begin{aligned}
\text{maximize} \quad & - \sum_{a \in Q_A} \frac{\mathsf{T}_A(a)}{N_{\mathbf{V}}} \cdot \log \left(\frac{\mathsf{T}_A(a)}{N_{\mathbf{V}}} \right) \\
\text{subject to} \quad & \underset{a \in Q_A}{\forall} \; \mathsf{T}_A(a) \geq 0 \\
& \underset{V_i \in \mathbf{V}}{\forall} \; \underset{a' \in Q_{V_i \cap A}}{\forall} \; \mathsf{T}_{V_i}(a') = \mathsf{T}_A(a').
\end{aligned}
$$

In the above, $N_{\mathbf{V}}$ denotes the total count obtained from any $V_i \in \mathbf{V}$. Since all views are consistent, the value should be the same for any V_i.

Experiments done in Qardaji et al. [2014] suggest using the maximum entropy approach.

6.3.3 CONSISTENCY BETWEEN NOISY VIEWS

The consistency problem is the main motivation behind the Fourier method in Barak et al. [2007]; however, a better solution is to use constrained inferencing as follows. The input to this step is a set of noisy marginal tables T_{V_i}, one for each set of attributes in the view set $\mathbf{V}$. The output is perturbed versions of these tables that are mutually consistent.

Mutual Consistency on a Set of Attributes. We first describe the method of ensuring that a set of view marginals is consistent on its common set of the attributes. Consider, wlog, views $V_1, \cdots, V_j$, let $A = V_1 \cap \ldots \cap V_j$. We want to ensure that $\mathsf{T}_{V_1}[A] \equiv \cdots \equiv \mathsf{T}_{V_j}[A]$. The goal is to make sure that $\mathsf{T}_{V_x}(a) = \mathsf{T}_{V_y}(a)$ for any two views $V_x, V_y \in \{V_1, V_2, \cdots, V_j\}$.

Here we apply the consistency techniques proposed in Hay et al. [2010], and achieve consistency in two steps. The first step is to compute the best approximation for the marginal table T_A. Assuming that all $T(V_i)$'s are constructed using the same privacy budget, and that $|V_1| = \cdots = |V_j|$, then for any $a \in Q_A$, the best approximation of $T_A(a)$ that minimizes the variance of the noise is the arithmetic mean of the value from all views, i.e.:

$$T_A(a) = \frac{1}{j} \sum_{i=1}^{j} T_{V_i}(a). \tag{6.6}$$

The second step is to update all T_{V_i}'s to be consistent with T_A. One can view T_A as a set of $2^{|A|}$ mutually exclusive constraints on all the entries in T_{V_i}. For each constraint $c \in Q_A$, do

$$T_{V_i}(c) \leftarrow T_{V_i}(c) + \frac{T_A(a) - T_{V_i}(a)}{2^{|V_i|-|A|}},$$

where a is the query c restricted to attributes in A.

The following example illustrates mutual consistency between $T_{V_1=\{a_1,a_2\}}$ and $T_{V_2=\{a_1,a_3\}}$.

$T_{V_1=\{a_1,a_2\}}$ before consistency	0.3	0.3	0.3	0.1
$T_{V_2=\{a_1,a_3\}}$ before consistency	0.2	0.3	0.1	0.4
T_{V_1} projected on a_1	0.6		0.4	
T_{V_2} projected on a_1	0.5		0.5	
best estimate of $T_{\{a_1\}}$	0.55		0.45	
$T_{V_1=\{a_1,a_2\}}$ after consistency	0.275	0.275	0.325	0.125
$T_{V_2=\{a_1,a_3\}}$ after consistency	0.225	0.325	0.075	0.375
T_{V_1} projected on a_2 is unchanged	0.6		0.4	
T_{V_2} projected on a_3 is unchanged	0.3		0.7	

Note that after mutual consistency, $T_{V_1=\{a_1,a_2\}}$ and $T_{V_2=\{a_1,a_3\}}$ agree on $\{a_1\}$ without changing the marginals of attributes not involved in the consistency.

Overall Consistency. We now describe how to ensure that all marginals are consistent on all subsets of attributes by performing a series of mutual consistency steps. The challenge here is to determine the order with which to perform the mutual consistency procedure. Suppose that we first make T_{V_1} and T_{V_2} consistent on the attribute set $V_1 \cap V_2 = \{a_1, a_2\}$, and then make T_{V_1} and T_{V_3} consistent on the attribute set $V_1 \cap V_3 = \{a_1, a_3\}$. This second step may make T_{V_1} and T_{V_2} inconsistent, because it may change the distribution of the attribute $\{a_1\}$. We note, however, if we have already made V_1, V_2, V_3 consistent on $\{a_1\}$, then the second step will not invalidate the consistency established in step 1. This is formalized in the following lemma.

Lemma 6.2 *If T_{V_1} and T_{V_2} are already consistent on $A \subset V_1 \cap V_2$, then enforcing mutual consistency between T_{V_1} and T_{V_2} does not change the projection of T_{V_1} on any subset of $(V_1 \setminus V_2) \cup A$.*

Proof. When updating T_{V_1} to affect the distribution of attributes in $V_1 \cap V_2$, increase to some cells in T_{V_1} must be balanced by equal amount of subtraction to other cells. When projecting T_{V_1} onto any subset of $(V_1 \setminus V_2) \cup A$, these changes cancel out. □

Utilizing Lemma 6.2, the following procedure ensures overall consistency. Take all sets of attributes that are the result of the intersection of some subset of $\mathbf{V}$; these sets form a partial order under the subset relation. One then obtains a topological sort of these sets, starting from the empty set. For each set A, one finds all views that include A, and ensures that these views are consistent on A. Note that consistency on the empty set of attributes ensures that the total counts in all marginals are the same, and this is done first. Following this order, a later consistency step will not invalidate consistency established in previous steps. Furthermore, following any topological order will result in the same result.

Accuracy Through Ripple Non-Negativity.   Noisy marginals may contain negative numbers. Since all entries in the true marginals are non-negative, one should change these negative numbers to 0. Intuitively this will improve the accuracy. However, experimental results have found that simply changing negative numbers to 0 dramatically increases the error. We believe that this is because the noisy answer for any query that includes cells that have low true counts is positively biased, because negative noises are partially removed, but positive noises remain. At the same time, the noisy answer for a query that does not include cells with low true counts does not have such a bias.

To avoid such bias, the following "Ripple" non-negativity method can be applied. This method turns negative counts into 0 while decreasing the counts for its neighbors to maintain overall count unchanged. Given an ℓ-way marginal table, for any entry that has count $c < -\theta$ for some small value of θ, we set the entry to 0 and subtract $|c|/\ell$ from each of its ℓ neighboring cells (i.e., cells obtained by flipping one of the ℓ bits). As doing this may result in other cells to be below $-\theta$, this is iterated until no cell is below $-\theta$. As each iteration distributes a negative count into ℓ neighbors, it is guaranteed to terminate quickly.

Qardaji et al. [2014] suggested only conducting one round of non-negativity step, as multiple rounds produce negligible additional improvements. Instead, Consistency + Non-negativity + Consistency was recommended.

6.3.4   CHOOSING A SET OF VIEWS

Obviously it is desirable to have every attribute appear in at least one view; otherwise, information about that attribute is not present, and the estimation has to assume that it is equally likely to be 1 or 0, which may turn out to be very inaccurate. Going beyond covering every single attribute, it is natural to ensure that every pair of attributes is covered in some view, and then every triple of attributes, and so on. Thus one approach is to first decide whether to cover all pairs or all triples, and then take advantage of the following concept from combinatorics theory.

Definition 6.3   Covering Design.   A (w, ℓ, t)-covering design of a set P is a collection of w subsets of P, each of which contains ℓ elements and is called a block, such that any t-element subset of P is contained in at least one block. An *optimal* (w, ℓ, t)-covering design minimizes the number of blocks.

Clearly, for a fixed P and t, the larger the ℓ, the smaller the w needs to be. We need a method to choose w, ℓ, t.

Setting $\ell = 8$. Qardaji et al. [2014] recommend choosing $\ell = 8$ (or values close to it, such as between 7 and 11). There are two sources of errors for any marginal generated by PriView: noise error, which is due to Laplacian noise added to satisfy differential privacy, and coverage error, which occurs when the marginal is not fully covered by any view.

To compute the noise error, we consider the result of reconstructing a pair of attributes. When choosing a set of w views of length ℓ each, reconstructing a pair from a single view that covers it has ESE of, $2^\ell w^2 \frac{2}{\epsilon^2}$. However, on average we expect a pair to be covered by $\frac{w\ell(\ell-1)}{d(d-1)}$ views, since there are $\frac{d(d-1)}{2}$ pairs, and these views include $\frac{w\ell(\ell-1)}{2}$ pairs. Averaging will reduce the ESE; thus the normalized error (after dividing N) is on the order of

$$err = \frac{1}{N} \sqrt{\frac{\frac{2^{\ell+1} w^2}{\epsilon^2}}{\frac{w\ell(\ell-1)}{d(d-1)}}} = \frac{2^{\frac{\ell+1}{2}}}{N\epsilon} \sqrt{\frac{wd(d-1)}{\ell(\ell-1)}}. \tag{6.7}$$

We want to choose ℓ to minimize (6.7). We are given N, d, ϵ, and can choose w and ℓ. We observe that w and ℓ are interdependent. When we compare covering designs with similar coverage, we can assume that they have roughly the same number of pairs, and thus $w \propto \frac{1}{\ell(\ell-1)}$. Then choosing ℓ to minimize (6.7) can be achieved by minimizing $\frac{2^{\ell/2}}{\ell(\ell-1)}$. A similar analysis for noise error of reconstructing triples require minimizing $\frac{2^{\ell/2}}{\ell(\ell-1)(\ell-2)}$. Choosing $\ell = 8$ works well, as can be seen from the following table.

ℓ	$\frac{2^{\ell/2}}{\ell(\ell-1)}$	$\frac{2^{\ell/2}}{\ell(\ell-1)(\ell-2)}$	ℓ	$\frac{2^{\ell/2}}{\ell(\ell-1)}$	$\frac{2^{\ell/2}}{\ell(\ell-1)(\ell-2)}$
5	0.283	0.094	9	0.314	0.045
6	0.267	0.067	10	0.356	0.044
7	0.269	0.054	11	0.411	0.046
8	0.286	0.048	12	0.485	0.048

It is interesting to know that the choice of ℓ is independent from N, d, ϵ, thus $\ell = 8$ can be used cross all settings.

Choosing t. Choosing the value for t does depend on N, d, ϵ. We observe that the overall error is affected by both the noise error and coverage error. Larger t provides better coverage, at the cost of higher noise error. We want to ensure that neither one is much larger than the other. The coverage error, however, cannot be analytically computed, as it depends on the nature of the dataset. It is high when there is high correlation among some attributes, which are not covered together. Empirically, we observe that choosing t so that the noise error falls in the range of 0.001 and 0.003 seems to work well.

Therefore, we find the best covering design with $\ell = 8$ for $t = 2, 3, 4$ and compute the error value from Equation (6.7). Many covering design solutions exist in online repositories such as Gordon [2012], from which we look up the covering designs for the desired N, t, ℓ value and find the design as well as the value w. Computing the noise error using (6.7) also requires N, for which a rough estimate suffices. For example, one could use a very small privacy budget, say, $\epsilon = 0.001$ to obtain a noisy count for it.

6.3.5   SPACE AND TIME COMPLEXITY

The space complexity of the PriView approach is the set of views, i.e., $w2^\ell$, which is quite small.

The time complexity for publishing the synopsis consists of the following three steps: First, constructing noisy views takes time $O(wN + w2^\ell)$. Second, the time complexity of the consistency step is determined by how many mutual consistency steps are taken, and how many views are involved in each step. The non-negativity step has time complexity $O(w2^\ell)$. The time to reconstruct one k-way marginal is determined by the convex optimization procedure with 2^k variables.

6.4   BIBLIOGRAPHICAL NOTES

Most of the content of this chapter is based on Qardaji et al. [2014]. The method combining the exponential mechanism and multiplicative update is presented in Hardt et al. [2012]. Barak et al. [2007] is the first paper studying the marginal publishing problem and introduced the Fourier method. See Thaler et al. [2012] as an example of learning-based methods.

CHAPTER 7

The Sparse Vector Technique

In this chapter we study the Sparse Vector Technique (SVT) which is a fundamental technique for satisfying differential privacy and has the unique quality that one can output some query answers without apparently paying any privacy cost. SVT has been used in both the interactive setting, where one tries to answer a sequence of queries that are not known ahead of the time, and in the non-interactive setting, where all queries are known.

7.1   INTRODUCTION

The Sparse vector technique is used to answer a sequence of queries with low sensitivity differentially privately and more accurately. It was first proposed by Dwork et al. [2009] and later refined in Roth and Roughgarden [2010] and Hardt and Rothblum [2010], and used in Chen et al. [2015], Gupta et al. [2012b], Lee and Clifton [2014], Shokri and Shmatikov [2015], Stoddard et al. [2014]. Compared with other techniques for satisfying DP, SVT has the unique quality that one can output some query answers without apparently paying any privacy cost. More specifically, in SVT one is given a sequence of queries and a certain threshold T, and outputs a vector indicating whether each query answer is above or below T; that is, the output is a vector $\{\bot, \top\}^{\ell}$, where ℓ is the number of queries answered, $\top$ indicates that the corresponding query answer is above the threshold and $\bot$ indicates below. SVT works by first perturbing the threshold T and then comparing each perturbed individual query answer against the noisy threshold. When we expect that the predominant majority of queries are on one side, e.g., below the threshold, we can use SVT so that while each output of $\top$ (which we call a **positive outcome**) consumes some privacy budget, each output of $\bot$ (**negative outcome**) consumes none. That is, with a fixed privacy budget and a given level of noise added to each query answer, one can keep answering queries as long as the number of $\top$'s does not exceed a pre-defined cutoff point.

This ability to avoid using any privacy budget for queries with negative outcomes is very powerful for **the interactive setting**, where one answers a sequence of queries without knowing ahead of time what these queries are. Some well-known lower-bound results Dinur and Nissim [2003], Dwork and Yekhanin [2008], Dwork et al. [2006, 2007] suggest that "one cannot answer a linear, in the database size, number of queries with small noise while preserving privacy" [Dwork et al., 2009]. This limitation can be bypassed using SVT, as in the iterative construction approach in Gupta et al. [2012b], Hardt and Rothblum [2010], Roth and Roughgarden [2010]. In this approach, one maintains a history of past queries and answers. For each new query, one first uses this history to derive an answer for the query, and then uses SVT to check whether the error of this derived answer is below a threshold. If it is, then one can use this derived answer for this new query without consuming any privacy budget. Only when the error of this derived answer is above the threshold would one need to spend the privacy budget accessing the database to answer the query.

With the power of SVT comes the subtlety of why it is private and the difficulty of applying it correctly. The version of SVT used in Gupta et al. [2012b], Hardt and Rothblum [2010], which was abstracted into a generic technique and described in lecture notes Roth [2011], turned out to be not differentially private as claimed. This error in Gupta et al. [2012b], Hardt and Rothblum [2010] is arguably not critical because it is possible to use a fixed version of SVT without affecting the main asymptotic results. Since 2014, several variants of SVT were developed; they were used for frequent itemset mining [Lee and Clifton, 2014], for feature selection in private classification [Stoddard et al., 2014], and for publishing high-dimensional data [Chen et al., 2015]. These usages are in the **non-interactive setting**, where all the queries are known ahead of the time, and the goal is to find c queries that have larger values, e.g., finding the c most frequent itemsets. Unfortunately, these variants do not satisfy DP, as pointed out in Chen and Machanavajjhala [2015]. When using a correct version of SVT in these papers, one would get significantly worse accuracy. Since these papers seek to improve the tradeoff between privacy and utility, the results in them are thus invalid.

The fact that many usages of SVT are not private, even when proofs of their privacy were given, is already known [Chen and Machanavajjhala, 2015, Zhang et al., 2014b]; however, we feel that what led to the erroneous proofs were not clearly explained, and such an explanation can help researchers to avoid similar errors in the future. One piece of evidence of the continuing confusion over SVT appears in Chen and Machanavajjhala [2015], the first paper that identifies errors in some SVT variants. In Chen and Machanavajjhala [2015], the SVT variants in Chen et al. [2015], Lee and Clifton [2014], Stoddard et al. [2014] were modeled as a generalized private threshold testing algorithm (GPTT), and a proof showing that GPTT does not satisfy ϵ-DP for any finite ϵ (which we use ∞-DP to denote in this paper) was given. However, as we show in this paper, the proof in Chen and Machanavajjhala [2015] was incorrect. This error was not reported in the literature. This chapter is to clearly explain why correct usages of SVT are private, and what are the most likely confusions that caused the myriad of incorrect usages of SVT.

A version of SVT with a correct privacy proof appeared in Dwork and Roth [2013], and was used in some recent work, e.g., Shokri and Shmatikov [2015]. To improve the accuracy of SVT, this chapter presents a version of SVT that adds less noise for the same level of privacy. In addition, this chapter develops a technique that optimizes the privacy budget allocation between that for perturbing the threshold and that for perturbing the query answers, and experimentally demonstrates its effectiveness.

This chapter also points out that usage of SVT can be replaced by the Exponential Mechanism (EM) [McSherry and Talwar, 2007] when used in the non-interactive setting. Most recent usages of SVT in Chen et al. [2015], Lee and Clifton [2014], Shokri and Shmatikov [2015],

Stoddard et al. [2014] are in the non-interactive setting, where the goal is to select up to c queries with the highest answers. In this setting, one could also use EM [McSherry and Talwar, 2007] c times to achieve the same objective, each time selecting the query with the highest answer. Using analysis as well as experiments, we demonstrate that EM outperforms SVT.

7.2   VARIANTS OF SVT

In this section, we analyze variants of SVT; six of them are listed in Figure 7.1. Algorithm 7.1 is an instantiation of our proposed SVT. Algorithm 7.2 is the version taken from Dwork and Roth [2013]. Algorithms 7.3, 7.4, 7.5, and 7.6 are taken from Chen et al. [2015], Lee and Clifton [2014], Roth [2011], Stoddard et al. [2014], respectively.

The table in Figure 7.2 summarizes the differences among these algorithms. Their privacy properties are given in the last row of the table. Algorithms 7.1 and 7.2 satisfy ϵ-DP, and the rest of them do not. Alg. 7.3, 7.5, 7.6 do not satisfy ϵ-DP for any finite ϵ, which we denote as ∞-DP.

An important input parameter to any SVT algorithm is the number c, i.e., how many positive outcomes one can answer before stopping. This number can be quite large. For example, in privately finding top-c frequent itemsets [Lee and Clifton, 2014], c ranges from 50–400. In using selective stochastic gradient descent to train deep learning models privately [Shokri and Shmatikov, 2015], the number of gradients to upload at each epoch ranges from 15–140,106.

To understand the differences between these variants, one can view SVT as having the following four steps:

1. Generate the threshold noise ρ (Line 1 in each algorithm), which will be added to the threshold during comparison between each query and the threshold (line 5). In all except Alg. 7.2, ρ scales with Δ/ϵ_1. In Alg. 7.2, however, ρ scales with $c\Delta/\epsilon_1$. This extra factor of c in the noise scale causes Alg. 7.2 to be much less accurate than Alg. 7.1. We show that including the factor of c is an effect of Alg. 7.2's design to resample ρ each time a query results in a positive outcome (Line 6). When keeping ρ unchanged, ρ does not need to scale with c to achieve privacy.

2. For each query q_i, generate noise ν_i to be added to the query (Line 4), which should scale with $2c\Delta/\epsilon_2$. In Alg. 7.4 and 7.6, ν_i scales with Δ/ϵ_2. Removing the factor of c from the magnitude of the noise will result in better utility; however, this is done at the cost of being non-private. Alg. 7.5 adds no noise to q_i at all, and is also non-private.

3. Compare the perturbed query answer with the noisy threshold and output whether it is above or below the threshold (Lines 5, 6, 9). Here Alg. 7.1 differs in that it outputs the noisy query answer $q_i(D) + \nu_i$, instead of an indicator $\top$. This makes it non-private.

4. Keep track of the number of $\top$'s in the output, and stop when one has outputted c $\top$'s (Line 7). This step is missed in Alg. 7.5 and 7.6. Without this limitation, one can answer as

Input/Output shared by all SVT Algorithms

Input: A private database D, a stream of queries $Q = q_1, q_2, \cdots$ each with sensitivity no more than Δ, either a sequence of thresholds $\mathbf{T} = T_1, T_2, \cdots$ or a single threshold T (see footnote *), and c, the maximum number of queries to be answered with $\top$.

Output: A stream of answers $a_1, a_2, \cdots$, where each $a_i \in \{\top, \bot\} \cup \mathbb{R}$ and $\mathbb{R}$ denotes the set of all real numbers.

Algorithm 7.1 An instantiation of the SVT proposed in this paper.

Input: $D, Q, \Delta, \mathbf{T} = T_1, T_2, \cdots, c.$
1: $\epsilon_1 = \epsilon/2, \quad \rho = \mathsf{Lap}\,(\Delta/\epsilon_1)$
2: $\epsilon_2 = \epsilon - \epsilon_1, \quad \text{count} = 0$
3: **for** each query $q_i \in Q$ **do**
4:      $v_i = \mathsf{Lap}\,(2c\Delta/\epsilon_2)$
5:      **if** $q_i(D) + v_i \geq T_i + \rho$ **then**
6:          Output $a_i = \top$
7:          count = count + 1, **Abort** if count $\geq c$.
8:      **else**
9:          Output $a_i = \bot$
10:     **end if**
11: **end for**

Algorithm 7.2 SVT in   Dwork and Roth [2013].

Input: $D, Q, \Delta, T, c.$
1: $\epsilon_1 = \epsilon/2, \quad \rho = \mathsf{Lap}\,(c\Delta/\epsilon_1)$
2: $\epsilon_2 = \epsilon - \epsilon_1, \quad \text{count} = 0$
3: **for** each query $q_i \in Q$ **do**
4:      $v_i = \mathsf{Lap}\,(2c\Delta/\epsilon_1)$
5:      **if** $q_i(D) + v_i \geq T + \rho$ **then**
6:          Output $a_i = \top, \rho = \mathsf{Lap}\,(c\Delta/\epsilon_2)$
7:          count = count + 1, **Abort** if count $\geq c$.
8:      **else**
9:          Output $a_i = \bot$
10:     **end if**
11: **end for**

Algorithm 7.3 SVT in Roth [2011].

Input: $D, Q, \Delta, T, c.$
1: $\epsilon_1 = \epsilon/2, \quad \rho = \mathsf{Lap}\,(\Delta/\epsilon_1),$
2: $\epsilon_2 = \epsilon - \epsilon_1, \quad \text{count} = 0$
3: **for** each query $q_i \in Q$ **do**
4:      $v_i = \mathsf{Lap}\,(c\Delta/\epsilon_2)$
5:      **if** $q_i(D) + v_i \geq T + \rho$ **then**
6:          Output $a_i = q_i(D) + v_i$
7:          count = count + 1, **Abort** if count $\geq c$.
8:      **else**
9:          Output $a_i = \bot$
10:     **end if**
11: **end for**

Algorithm 7.4 SVT in Lee and Clifton [2014].

Input: $D, Q, \Delta, T, c.$
1: $\epsilon_1 = \epsilon/4, \quad \rho = \mathsf{Lap}\,(\Delta/\epsilon_1)$
2: $\epsilon_2 = \epsilon - \epsilon_1, \quad \text{count} = 0$
3: **for** each query $q_i \in Q$ **do**
4:      $v_i = \mathsf{Lap}\,(\Delta/\epsilon_2)$
5:      **if** $q_i(D) + v_i \geq T + \rho$ **then**
6:          Output $a_i = \top$
7:          count = count + 1, **Abort** if count $\geq c$.
8:      **else**
9:          Output $a_i = \bot$
10:     **end if**
11: **end for**

Figure 7.1: A selection of SVT variants.

Algorithm 7.5 SVT in Stoddard et al. [2014].	**Algorithm 7.6** SVT in Chen et al. [2015].
Input: D, Q, Δ, T.	**Input:** $D, Q, \Delta, \mathbf{T} = T_1, T_2, \cdots$.
1: $\epsilon_1 = \epsilon/2, \quad \rho = \mathsf{Lap}(\Delta/\epsilon_1)$	1: $\epsilon_1 = \epsilon/2, \quad \rho = \mathsf{Lap}(\Delta/\epsilon_1)$
2: $\epsilon_2 = \epsilon - \epsilon_1$	2: $\epsilon_2 = \epsilon - \epsilon_1$
3: **for** each query $q_i \in Q$ **do**	3: **for** each query $q_i \in Q$ **do**
4: $\quad v_i = 0$	4: $\quad v_i = \mathsf{Lap}(\Delta/\epsilon_2)$
5: $\quad$ **if** $q_i(D) + v_i \geq T + \rho$ **then**	5: $\quad$ **if** $q_i(D) + v_i \geq T_i + \rho$ **then**
6: $\quad\quad$ Output $a_i = \top$	6: $\quad\quad$ Output $a_i = \top$
7:	7:
8: $\quad$ **else**	8: $\quad$ **else**
9: $\quad\quad$ Output $a_i = \bot$	9: $\quad\quad$ Output $a_i = \bot$
10: $\quad$ **end if**	10: $\quad$ **end if**
11: **end for**	11: **end for**

	Alg. 7.1	**Alg. 7.2**	**Alg. 7.3**	**Alg. 7.4**	**Alg. 7.5**	**Alg. 7.6**
ϵ_1	$\epsilon/2$	$\epsilon/2$	$\epsilon/2$	$\epsilon/4$	$\epsilon/2$	$\epsilon/2$
Scale of threshold noise ρ	Δ/ϵ_1	$c\Delta/\epsilon_1$	Δ/ϵ_1	Δ/ϵ_1	Δ/ϵ_1	Δ/ϵ_1
Reset ρ after each output of $\top$ **(unnecessary)**		Yes				
Scale of query noise v_i	$2c\Delta/\epsilon_2$	$2c\Delta/\epsilon_2$	$c\Delta/\epsilon_2$	Δ/ϵ_2	0	Δ/ϵ_2
Outputting $q_i + v_i$ instead of $\top$ **(not private)**			Yes			
Outputting unbounded $\top$'s **(not private)**					Yes	Yes
Privacy Property	ϵ-DP	ϵ-DP	∞-DP	$\left(\frac{1+6c}{4}\epsilon\right)$-DP	∞-DP	∞-DP

Figure 7.2: Differences among Algorithms 7.1–7.6

* Algorithms 7.1 and 7.6 use a sequence of thresholds $\mathbf{T} = T_1, T_2, \cdots$, allowing different thresholds for different queries. The other algorithms use the same threshold T for all queries. We point out that this difference is mostly syntactical. In fact, having an SVT where the threshold always equals 0 suffices. Given a sequence of queries $q_1, q_2, \cdots$, and a sequence of thresholds $\mathbf{T} = T_1, T_2, \cdots$, we can define a new sequence of queries $r_i = q_i - T_i$, and apply the SVT to r_i using 0 as the threshold to obtain the same result. In this paper, we decide to use thresholds to be consistent with the existing papers.

** ∞-DP means that an algorithm doesn't satisfy ϵ'-DP for any finite privacy budget ϵ'.

many queries as there are with a fixed accuracy level for each query. If this was to be private, then one obtains privacy kind of "for free."

7.2.1 PRIVACY PROOF FOR PROPOSED SVT

We now prove the privacy of Algorithm 7.1. We break down the proof into two steps, to make the proof easier to understand, and, more importantly, to enable us to point out what confusions likely cause the different non-private variants of SVT to be proposed. In the first step, we analyze the situation where the output is $\perp^\ell$, a length-ℓ vector $\langle \perp, \cdots, \perp \rangle$, indicating that all ℓ queries are tested to be below the threshold.

Lemma 7.1 *Let $\mathcal{A}$ be Algorithm 7.1. For any neighboring datasets D and D', and any integer ℓ, we have*

$$\Pr\left[\mathcal{A}(D) = \perp^\ell\right] \le e^{\frac{\epsilon}{2}}\Pr\left[\mathcal{A}(D') = \perp^\ell\right].$$

Proof. We have

$$\Pr\left[\mathcal{A}(D) = \perp^\ell\right] = \int_{-\infty}^{\infty} \Pr\left[\rho = z\right] f_D(z)\, dz,$$

$$\text{where } f_D(z) = \Pr\left[\mathcal{A}(D) = \perp^\ell \mid \rho = z\right] \tag{7.1}$$

$$= \prod_{i \in \{1,2,\cdots,\ell\}} \Pr\left[q_i(D) + v_i < T_i + z\right]. \tag{7.2}$$

The probability of outputting $\perp^\ell$ over D is the summation (or integral) of the product of $\Pr[\rho = z]$, the probability that the threshold noise equals z, and $f_D(z)$, the conditional probability that $\perp^\ell$ is the output on D given that the threshold noise ρ is z. The step from (7.1) to (7.2) is because, given D, $\mathbf{T}$, the queries, and ρ, whether one query results in $\perp$ or not depends completely on the noise v_i and is independent from whether any other query results in $\perp$.

The key observation underlying the SVT technique is that for any neighboring D, D', we have $f_D(z) \le f_{D'}(z + \Delta)$. Suppose that we have $q_i(D) = q_i(D') - \Delta$ for each q_i, then the ratio $f_D(z)/f_{D'}(z)$ is unbounded when $|L|$ is unbounded. However, $f_D(z)$ is upper-bounded by the case where the dataset is D' but the noisy threshold **is increased by** Δ, because for any query q_i, $|q_i(D) - q_i(D')| \le \Delta$. More precisely, we have

$$\Pr\left[q_i(D) + v_i < T_i + z\right] = \Pr\left[v_i < T_i - q_i(D) + z\right]$$
$$\le \Pr\left[v_i < T_i + \Delta - q_i(D') + z\right]$$
$$= \Pr\left[q_i(D') + v_i < T_i + (z + \Delta)\right]. \tag{7.3}$$

Because $\rho = \mathsf{Lap}\left(\Delta/\epsilon_1\right)$, by the property of the Laplace distribution, we have:

$$\forall z, \ \Pr\left[\rho = z\right] \le e^{\epsilon_1}\Pr\left[\rho = z + \Delta\right], \text{ and thus}$$

$$\Pr\left[\mathcal{A}(D) = \bot^\ell\right] = \int_{-\infty}^{\infty} \Pr[\rho = z] \ f_D(z) \, dz$$

$$\leq \int_{-\infty}^{\infty} e^{\epsilon_1} \Pr[\rho = z + \Delta] \ f_{D'}(z + \Delta) \, dz$$

$$= e^{\epsilon_1} \int_{-\infty}^{\infty} \Pr[\rho = z'] \ f_{D'}(z') \, dz' \qquad \text{let } z' = z + \Delta$$

$$= e^{\epsilon_1} \Pr\left[\mathcal{A}(D') = \bot^\ell\right].$$

This proves the lemma. $\qquad\qquad\qquad\qquad\qquad\qquad\qquad\qquad\qquad\qquad\square$

We can obtain a similar result when the output is $\top^\ell$ instead of $\bot^\ell$, i.e., $\Pr\left[\mathcal{A}(D) = \top^\ell\right] \leq e^{\epsilon_1} \Pr\left[\mathcal{A}(D') = \top^\ell\right]$, because $\Pr[\rho = z] \leq e^{\epsilon_1} \Pr[\rho = z - \Delta]$ and $g_D(z) \leq g_{D'}(z - \Delta)$, where

$$g_D(z) = \prod_i \Pr[q_i(D) + v_i \geq T_i + z]. \tag{7.4}$$

The fact that this bounding technique works both for positive outputs and negative outputs likely contributes to the misunderstandings behind Alg. 7.5 and 7.6, which treat positive and negative outputs exactly the same way. The error is that when the output consists of both $\bot$ and $\top$, one has to choose one side (either positive or negative) to be bounded by the above technique, and cannot do both at the same time.

We also observe that the proof of Lemma 7.1 will go through if no noise is added to the query answers, i.e., $v_i = 0$, because Eq (7.3) holds even when $v_i = 0$. It is likely because of this observation that Alg. 7.5 adds no noise to query answers. However, when considering outcomes that include both positive answers ($\top$'s) and negative answers ($\bot$'s), one has to add noises to the query answers, as we show below.

Theorem 7.2 *Algorithm 7.1 is ϵ-DP.*

Proof. Consider any output vector $\vec{a} \in \{\bot, \top\}^\ell$. Let $\vec{a} = \langle a_1, \cdots, a_\ell \rangle$, $I_\top = \{i : a_i = \top\}$, and $I_\bot = \{i : a_i = \bot\}$. Clearly, $|I_\top| \leq c$. We have

$$\Pr\left[\mathcal{A}(D) = \vec{a}\right] = \int_{-\infty}^{\infty} \Pr[\rho = z] \ f_D(z) \ g_D(z) \, dz, \tag{7.5}$$

$$\text{where} \quad f_D(z) = \prod_{i \in I_\bot} \Pr[q_i(D) + v_i < T_i + z]$$

$$\text{and} \quad g_D(z) = \prod_{i \in I_\top} \Pr[q_i(D) + v_i \geq T_i + z].$$

The following, together with $\epsilon = \epsilon_1 + \epsilon_2$, prove this theorem:

$$\Pr[\rho = z] \le e^{\epsilon_1} \Pr[\rho = z + \Delta]$$
$$f_D(z) \le f_{D'}(z + \Delta) \tag{7.6}$$
$$g_D(z) \le e^{\epsilon_2} g_{D'}(z + \Delta). \tag{7.7}$$

Equation (7.6) deals with all the negative outcomes. Equation (7.7), which deals with positive outcomes, is ensured by several factors. At most c positive outcomes can occur, $|q_i(D) - q_i(D')| \le \Delta$, and the threshold for D' is just Δ higher than for D; thus adding noise $v_i = \mathsf{Lap}\,(2c\Delta/\epsilon_2)$ to each query ensures the desired bound. More precisely,

$$g_D(z) = \prod_{i \in I_\top} \Pr\left[v_i \ge T_i + z - q_i(D)\right]$$

$$\le \prod_{i \in I_\top} \Pr\left[v_i \ge T_i + z - \Delta - q_i(D')\right] \tag{7.8}$$

$$\le \prod_{i \in I_\top} e^{\epsilon_2/c} \Pr\left[v_i \ge T_i + z - \Delta - q_i(D') + 2\Delta\right] \tag{7.9}$$

$$\le e^{\epsilon_2} \prod_{i \in I_\top} \Pr\left[q_i(D') + v_i \ge T_i + z + \Delta\right] \tag{7.10}$$

$$= e^{\epsilon_2} g_{D'}(z + \Delta).$$

Equation (7.8) is because $-q_i(D) \ge -\Delta - q_i(D')$, Eq. (7.9) is from the Laplace distribution's property, and Eq. (7.10) is because there are at most c positive outcomes, i.e., $|I_\top| \le c$. □

We observe that while $g_D(z) \le g_{D'}(z - \Delta)$ is true, replacing (7.7) with it does not help us prove anything, because (7.6) uses $(z + \Delta)$ and (7.7) uses $(z - \Delta)$, and we cannot change the integration variable in a consistent way.

7.2.2 PRIVACY PROPERTIES OF OTHER VARIANTS

Algorithm 7.2 is taken from the differential privacy book published in 2014 [Dwork and Roth, 2013]. It is proven to be ϵ-DP. It has two differences when compared with Algorithm 7.1. First, ρ follows $\mathsf{Lap}\,(c\Delta/\epsilon_1)$ instead of $\mathsf{Lap}\,(\Delta/\epsilon_1)$, where c is the maximum number of $\top$'s the algorithm outputs. This causes Algorithm 7.2 to have significantly worse performance than Algorithm 7.1, as we show in Section 7.4.1. Second, Algorithm 7.2 refreshes the noisy threshold T after each output of $\top$. We note that making the threshold noise scale with c is necessary for privacy *only if* one refreshes the threshold noise after each output of $\top$; however, such refreshing is unnecessary.

Algorithm 7.3 is taken from Roth [2011], which in turn was abstracted from the algorithms used in Gupta et al. [2012b], Hardt and Rothblum [2010]. It has two differences from Algorithm 7.1. First, v_i follows $\mathsf{Lap}\,(c\Delta/\epsilon_2)$ instead of $\mathsf{Lap}\,(2c\Delta/\epsilon_1)$; this is not enough for ϵ-DP (even though it suffices for $\frac{3\epsilon}{2}$-DP). Second, it actually outputs the noisy query answer instead of $\top$ for a query above the threshold. This latter fact causes Algorithm 7.3 to be not ϵ'-DP for any finite ϵ'. A proof for this appeared in Appendix A of Zhang et al. [2014b]; for completeness, we also give the proof. But first, we want to point out that the error in the proof for Algorithm 7.3's privacy in Roth [2011] occurs in the following steps:

$$
\begin{aligned}
&\Pr\left[\mathcal{A}(D) = \vec{a}\right] \\
&= \int_{-\infty}^{\infty} \Pr\left[\rho = z\right] f_D(z) \prod_{i \in I_\top} \Pr\left[q_i(D) + v_i \geq T + z \wedge q_i(D) + v_i = a_i\right] dz \\
&= \int_{-\infty}^{\infty} \Pr\left[\rho = z\right] f_D(z) \prod_{i \in I_\top} \Pr\left[q_i(D) + v_i = a_i\right] dz \qquad (7.11) \\
&\leq \int_{-\infty}^{\infty} e^{\epsilon_1} \Pr\left[\rho = z + \Delta\right] f_{D'}(z + \Delta)\, dz \prod_{i \in I_\top} e^{\epsilon_2/c} \Pr\left[q_i(D') + v_i = a_i\right].
\end{aligned}
$$

The error occurs when going to (7.11), which is implicitly done in Roth [2011]. This step removes the condition $q_i(D) + v_i \geq T + z$.

Another way to look at this error is that outputting the positive query answers reveals information about the noisy threshold, since the noisy threshold must be below the outputted query answer. Once information about the noisy threshold is leaked, the ability to answer each negative query "for free" disappears.

Theorem 7.3   *Algorithm 7.3 is not ϵ'-DP for any finite ϵ'.*

Proof. Set $c = 1$ for simplicity. Given any finite $\epsilon' > 0$, we construct an example to show that Algorithm 7.3 is not ϵ'-DP. Consider an example with $T = 0$, and $m + 1$ queries $\mathbf{q}$ with sensitivity Δ such that $\mathbf{q}(D) = 0^m \Delta$ and $\mathbf{q}(D') = \Delta^m 0$, and the output vector $\vec{a} = \bot^m 0$, that is, only the last query answer is a numeric value 0. Let $\mathcal{A}$ be Algorithm 7.3. We show that $\frac{\Pr[\mathcal{A}(D) = \vec{a}]}{\Pr[\mathcal{A}(D') = \vec{a}]} \geq e^{\epsilon'}$ for any $\epsilon' > 0$ when m is large enough.

We denote the cumulative distribution function of $\mathsf{Lap}\left(\frac{2\Delta}{\epsilon}\right)$ by $F(x)$. We have

$$
\begin{aligned}
&\Pr\left[\mathcal{A}(D) = \vec{a}\right] \\
&= \int_{-\infty}^{\infty} \Pr\left[\rho = z\right] f_D(z) \Pr\left[\Delta + v_{m+1} \geq z \wedge \Delta + v_{m+1} = 0\right] dz \\
&= \int_{-\infty}^{\infty} \Pr\left[\rho = z\right] f_D(z) \Pr\left[0 \geq z\right] \Pr\left[v_{m+1} = -\Delta\right] dz
\end{aligned}
$$

$$= \frac{\epsilon}{4\Delta} e^{-\frac{\epsilon}{2}} \int_{-\infty}^{\infty} \Pr[\rho = z] \, f_D(z) \Pr[0 \geq z] \, dz$$

$$= \frac{\epsilon}{4\Delta} e^{-\frac{\epsilon}{2}} \int_{-\infty}^{0} \Pr[\rho = z] \, f_D(z) \, dz$$

$$= \frac{\epsilon}{4\Delta} e^{-\frac{\epsilon}{2}} \int_{-\infty}^{0} \Pr[\rho = z] \prod_{i=1}^{m} \Pr[v_i < z] \, dz$$

$$= \frac{\epsilon}{4\Delta} e^{-\frac{\epsilon}{2}} \int_{-\infty}^{0} \Pr[\rho = z] \, (F(z))^m \, dz, \tag{7.12}$$

and similarly

$$\Pr\left[\mathcal{A}(D') = \vec{a}\right] = \frac{\epsilon}{4\Delta} \int_{-\infty}^{0} \Pr[\rho = z'] \, (F(z' - \Delta))^m \, dz'. \tag{7.13}$$

The fact that 0 is given as an output reveals the information that the noisy threshold is at most 0, forcing the range of integration to be from $-\infty$ to 0, instead of from $-\infty$ to ∞. This prevents the use of changing z in (7.12) to $z' - \Delta$ to bound the ratio of (7.12) to (7.13). Noting that $\frac{F(z)}{F(z-\Delta)} = e^{\frac{\epsilon}{2}}$ for any $z \leq 0$, we thus have

$$\frac{\Pr\left[\mathcal{A}(D) = \vec{a}\right]}{\Pr\left[\mathcal{A}(D') = \vec{a}\right]} = e^{-\frac{\epsilon}{2}} \frac{\int_{-\infty}^{0} \Pr[\rho = z] \, (F(z))^m \, dz}{\int_{-\infty}^{0} \Pr[\rho = z'] \, (F(z' - \Delta))^m \, dz'}$$

$$= e^{-\frac{\epsilon}{2}} \frac{\int_{-\infty}^{0} \Pr[\rho = z] \, (e^{\frac{\epsilon}{2}} F(z - \Delta))^m \, dz}{\int_{-\infty}^{0} \Pr[\rho = z'] \, (F(z' - \Delta))^m \, dz'}$$

$$= e^{(m-1)\frac{\epsilon}{2}},$$

and thus when $m > \lceil \frac{2\epsilon'}{\epsilon} \rceil + 1$, we have $\frac{\Pr[\mathcal{A}(D)=\vec{a}]}{\Pr[\mathcal{A}(D')=\vec{a}]} > e^{\epsilon'}$. $\square$

Algorithm 7.4, taken from Lee and Clifton [2014], differs from Algorithm 7.1 in the following ways. First, it sets ϵ_1 to be $\epsilon/4$ instead of $\epsilon/2$. This has no impact on the privacy. Second, v_i does not scale with c. As a result, Algorithm 7.4 is only $\left(\frac{1+6c}{4}\right)\epsilon$-DP in general. In Lee and Clifton [2014], Algorithm 7.4 is applied for finding frequent itemsets, where the queries are counting queries and are monotonic. Because of this monotonicity, the usage of Algorithm 7.4 here is $\left(\frac{1+3c}{4}\right)\epsilon$-DP. Theorem 7.6 can be applied to Algorithm 7.4 to establish this privacy property; we thus omit the proof of this.

Algorithm 7.6, taken from Chen et al. [2015], was motivated by the observation that the proof in Lee and Clifton [2014] can go through without stopping after encountering c positive outcomes, and removed this limitation.

Alg 7.5, taken from Stoddard et al. [2014], further used the observation that the derivation of Lemma 7.1 does not depend on the addition of noises, and removed that part as well. The proofs for Algorithms 7.4, 7.5, and 7.6 in Chen et al. [2015], Lee and Clifton [2014], Stoddard et al. [2014] roughly use the logic below.

$$\int_{-\infty}^{\infty} \Pr\left[\rho = z\right] f_D(z) g_D(z) dz \leq e^{\epsilon} \int_{-\infty}^{\infty} \Pr\left[\rho = z\right] f_{D'}(z) g_{D'}(z) dz$$

$$\text{because } \int_{-\infty}^{\infty} \Pr\left[\rho = z\right] f_D(z)\, dz \leq e^{\epsilon/2} \int_{-\infty}^{\infty} \Pr\left[\rho = z\right]\, f_{D'}(z)\, dz$$

$$\text{and } \int_{-\infty}^{\infty} \Pr\left[\rho = z\right] g_D(z)\, dz \leq e^{\epsilon/2} \int_{-\infty}^{\infty} \Pr\left[\rho = z\right] g_{D'}(z).$$

This logic incorrectly assumes the following is true:

$$\int_{-\infty}^{\infty} p(z) f(z) g(z) dz = \int_{-\infty}^{\infty} p(z) f(z) dz \int_{-\infty}^{\infty} p(z) g(z) dz.$$

A proof that Algorithm 7.6 does not satisfy ϵ-DP for any finite ϵ is given in Appendix B of Zhang et al. [2014b]. Here we also present a proof in the following.

Theorem 7.4   *Algorithm 7.6 is not ϵ'-DP for any finite ϵ'.*

Proof. We construct a counterexample with $\Delta = 1$, $T = 0$, and $2m$ queries such that $\mathbf{q}(D) = 0^{2m}$, and $\mathbf{q}(D') = 1^m(-1)^m$. Consider the output vector $\vec{a} = \perp^m \top^m$. Denote the cumulative distribution function of v_i by $F(x)$. From Eq (7.5), We have

$$\Pr\left[\mathcal{A}(D) = \vec{a}\right]$$
$$= \int_{-\infty}^{\infty} \Pr\left[\rho = z\right] \prod_{i=1}^{m} \Pr\left[0 + v_i < z\right] \prod_{i=m+1}^{2m} \Pr\left[0 + v_i \geq z\right]\, dz$$
$$= \int_{-\infty}^{\infty} \Pr\left[\rho = z\right] (F(z)(1 - F(z)))^m\, dz,$$

and

$$\Pr\left[\mathcal{A}(D') = \vec{a}\right]$$
$$= \int_{-\infty}^{\infty} \Pr\left[\rho = z\right] \prod_{i=1}^{m} \Pr\left[1 + v_i < z\right] \prod_{i=m+1}^{2m} \Pr\left[-1 + v_i \geq z\right]\, dz$$
$$= \int_{-\infty}^{\infty} \Pr\left[\rho = z\right] (F(z-1)(1 - F(z+1)))^m\, dz.$$

We now show that $\frac{\Pr[\mathcal{A}(D) = \vec{a}]}{\Pr[\mathcal{A}(D') = \vec{a}]}$ is unbounded as m increases, proving this theorem. Compare $F(z)(1 - F(z))$ with $F(z - 1)(1 - F(z + 1))$. Note that $F(z)$ is monotonically increasing. When $z \leq 0$,

$$\frac{F(z)(1 - F(z))}{F(z-1)(1 - F(z+1))} \geq \frac{F(z)}{F(z-1)} = \frac{\frac{1}{2} e^{\frac{\epsilon}{2} z}}{\frac{1}{2} e^{\frac{\epsilon}{2}(z-1)}} = e^{\frac{\epsilon}{2}}.$$

When $z > 0$, we also have

$$\frac{F(z)(1 - F(z))}{F(z - 1)(1 - F(z + 1))} \geq \frac{1 - F(z)}{1 - F(z + 1)} = \frac{\frac{1}{2}e^{-\frac{\epsilon}{2}z}}{\frac{1}{2}e^{-\frac{\epsilon}{2}(z+1)}} = e^{\frac{\epsilon}{2}}.$$

So, $\frac{\Pr[\mathcal{A}(D) = \vec{a}]}{\Pr[\mathcal{A}(D') = \vec{a}]} \geq e^{\frac{m\epsilon}{2}}$, which is greater than $e^{\epsilon'}$ when $m > \lceil \frac{2\epsilon'}{\epsilon} \rceil$ for any finite ϵ'.   □

While the proof also applies to Algorithm 7.5, we give a much simpler proof of this below.

Theorem 7.5   *Algorithm 7.5 is not ϵ'-DP for any finite ϵ'.*

Proof. Consider a simple example, with $T = 0, \Delta = 1, \mathbf{q} = \langle q_1, q_2 \rangle$ such that $\mathbf{q}(D) = \langle 0, 1 \rangle$ and $\mathbf{q}(D') = \langle 1, 0 \rangle$, and $\vec{a} = \langle \perp, \top \rangle$. Then by Eq. (7.5), we have

$$\Pr\left[\mathcal{A}(D) = \vec{a}\right] = \int_{-\infty}^{\infty} \Pr[\rho = z] \Pr[0 < z] \Pr[1 \geq z] \, dz$$
$$= \int_0^1 \Pr[\rho = z] \, dz > 0,$$

which is nonzero; and

$$\Pr\left[\mathcal{A}(D') = \vec{a}\right] = \int_{-\infty}^{\infty} \Pr\left[\rho = z'\right] \Pr\left[1 < z'\right] \Pr\left[0 \geq z'\right] \, dz',$$

which is zero. So the probability ratio $\frac{\Pr[\mathcal{A}(D) = \vec{a}]}{\Pr[\mathcal{A}(D') = \vec{a}]} = \infty$.   □

7.2.3   ERROR IN PRIVACY ANALYSIS OF GPTT

In Chen and Machanavajjhala [2015], the SVT variants in Chen et al. [2015], Lee and Clifton [2014], Stoddard et al. [2014] were modeled as a generalized private threshold testing algorithm (GPTT). In GPTT, the threshold T is perturbed using $\rho = \mathsf{Lap}\,(\Delta/\epsilon_1)$ and each query answer is perturbed using $\mathsf{Lap}\,(\Delta/\epsilon_2)$ and there is no cutoff; thus GPTT can be viewed as a generalization of Algorithm 7.6. When setting $\epsilon_1 = \epsilon_2 = \frac{\epsilon}{2}$, GPTT becomes Algorithm 7.6.

There is a constructive proof in Chen and Machanavajjhala [2015] to show that GPTT is not ϵ'-DP for any finite ϵ'. However, this proof is incorrect. This error is quite subtle. We discovered the error only after observing that the technique of the proof can be applied to show that Algorithm 7.1 (which we have proved to be private) to be non-private. The detailed discussion of this error is quite technical, and is presented as follows.

The non-private proof in Chen and Machanavajjhala [2015] considered the counter-example with $\Delta = 1, T = 0$, a sequence $\mathbf{q}$ of $2t$ queries such that $\mathbf{q}(D) = 0^t 1^t$ and $\mathbf{q}(D') = 1^t 0^t$, and output vector $\vec{a} = \perp^t \mathsf{T}^t$. Then

$$\frac{\Pr\left[GPTT(D) = \vec{a}\right]}{\Pr\left[GPTT(D') = \vec{a}\right]} = \frac{\int_{-\infty}^{\infty} \Pr\left[\rho = z\right]\left(F_{\epsilon_2}(z) - F_{\epsilon_2}(z)F_{\epsilon_2}(z-1)\right)^t dz}{\int_{-\infty}^{\infty} \Pr\left[\rho = z\right]\left(F_{\epsilon_2}(z-1) - F_{\epsilon_2}(z)F_{\epsilon_2}(z-1)\right)^t dz}$$

where $\quad F_{\epsilon}(x)$ is the cumulative distribution function of $\mathsf{Lap}\,(1/\epsilon)$.

The goal of the proof is to show that the above is unbounded as t increases. A key observation is that the ratio of the integrands of the two integrals is always larger than 1, i.e.,

$$\kappa(z) = \frac{F_{\epsilon_2}(z) - F_{\epsilon_2}(z)F_{\epsilon_2}(z-1)}{F_{\epsilon_2}(z-1) - F_{\epsilon_2}(z)F_{\epsilon_2}(z-1)} > 1.$$

For example, since $F_{\epsilon}(x)$ is the cumulative distribution function of $\mathsf{Lap}\,(1/\epsilon)$, we have $F_{\epsilon_2}(0) = 1/2$ and $F_{\epsilon_2}(-1) < 1/2$; and thus $\kappa(0) = \frac{1 - F_{\epsilon_2}(-1)}{F_{\epsilon_2}(-1)} > 1$. However, when $|z|$ goes to ∞, $\kappa(z)$ goes to 1. Thus the proof tries to limit the integrals to be a finite interval so that there is a lower-bound for $\kappa(z)$ that is greater than 1. It denotes $\alpha = \Pr\left[GPTT(D') = \vec{a}\right]$. Then choose parameter $\delta = |F_{\epsilon_1}^{-1}(\frac{\alpha}{4})|$ to use $[-\delta, \delta]$ as the finite interval and thus

$$\alpha \le 2 \int_{-\delta}^{\delta} \Pr\left[\rho = z\right]\left(F_{\epsilon_2}(z-1) - F_{\epsilon_2}(z)F_{\epsilon_2}(z-1)\right)^t dz.$$

Denote the minimum of $\kappa(z)$ in the closed interval $[-\delta, \delta]$ by κ. Then we have $\frac{\Pr[GPTT(D) = \vec{a}]}{\Pr[GPTT(D') = \vec{a}]} > \frac{\kappa^t}{2}$. The proof claims that for any $\epsilon' > 1$ there exists a t to make the above ratio larger than $e^{\epsilon'}$.

The proof is incorrect because of dependency in the parameters. First, α is a function of t; and when t increases, α decreases because the integrand above is positive and decreasing. Second, δ depends on α, and when α decreases, δ increases. Thus when t increases, δ increases. We write δ as $\delta(t)$ to make the dependency on t explicit. Third, κ, the minimum value of $\kappa(z)$ over the interval $[-\delta(t), \delta(t)]$, decreases when t increases. That is, κ is also dependent on t, denoted by $\kappa(t)$, and decreases while t increases. It is not sure that there exists such a t that $\frac{\kappa(t)^t}{2} > e^{\epsilon'}$ for any $\epsilon' > 1$.

To demonstrate that the error in the proof cannot be easily fixed, we point out that following the logic of that proof, one can prove that Algorithm 7.1 is not ϵ'-DP for any finite ϵ'. We now show such a "proof" that contradicts Lemma 7.1. Let $\mathcal{A}$ be Algorithm 7.1, with $c = 1$. Consider an example with $\Delta = 1$, $T = 0$, a sequence $\mathbf{q}$ of t queries such that $\mathbf{q}(D) = 0^t$ and $\mathbf{q}(D') = 1^t$, and output vector $\vec{a} = \perp^t$. Let

$$\beta = \Pr\left[\mathcal{A}(D) = \perp^\ell\right] = \int_{-\infty}^{\infty} \Pr[\rho = z]\left(F_{\frac{\epsilon}{4}}(z)\right)^t dz$$

$$\alpha = \Pr\left[\mathcal{A}(D') = \perp^\ell\right] = \int_{-\infty}^{\infty} \Pr[\rho = z]\left(F_{\frac{\epsilon}{4}}(z-1)\right)^t dz,$$

where $F_{\frac{\epsilon}{4}}(x)$ is the cumulative distribution function of $\mathsf{Lap}\left(\dfrac{4}{\epsilon}\right)$.

Find such a parameter δ that $\int_{-\delta}^{\delta} \Pr[\rho = z]\, dz \geq 1 - \frac{\alpha}{2}$. Then $\int_{-\delta}^{\delta} \Pr[\rho = z]$ $\left(F_{\frac{\epsilon}{4}}(z-1)\right)^t dz \geq \frac{\alpha}{2}$. Let κ be the minimum value of $\dfrac{F_{\frac{\epsilon}{4}}(z)}{F_{\frac{\epsilon}{4}}(z-1)}$ in $[-\delta, \delta]$; it must be that $\kappa > 1$. Then

$$\beta > \int_{-\delta}^{\delta} \Pr[\rho = z]\left(F_{\frac{\epsilon}{4}}(z)\right)^t dz \geq \int_{-\delta}^{\delta} \Pr[\rho = z]\left(\kappa F_{\frac{\epsilon}{4}}(z-1)\right)^t dz$$

$$= \kappa^t \int_{-\delta}^{\delta} \Pr[\rho = z]\left(F_{\frac{\epsilon}{4}}(z-1)\right)^t dz \geq \frac{\kappa^t}{2}\alpha.$$

Since $\kappa > 1$, one can choose a large enough t to make $\frac{\beta}{\alpha} = \frac{\kappa^t}{2}$ to be as large as needed. We note that this contradicts Lemma 7.1. The contradiction shows that the proof logic used in Chen and Machanavajjhala [2015] is incorrect.

7.2.4 OTHER VARIANTS

Some usages of SVT aim at satisfying (ϵ, δ)-DP [Dwork et al., 2006], instead of ϵ-DP. These often exploit the advanced composition theorem for DP [Dwork et al., 2010], which states that applying k instances of ϵ-DP algorithms satisfies (ϵ', δ')-DP, where $\epsilon' = \sqrt{2k \ln(1/\delta')}\epsilon + k\epsilon(e^\epsilon - 1)$. In this paper, we limit our attention to SVT variants to those satisfying ϵ-DP, which are what have been used in the data mining community [Chen et al., 2015, Lee and Clifton, 2014, Shokri and Shmatikov, 2015, Stoddard et al., 2014].

The SVT used in Hardt and Rothblum [2010], Roth and Roughgarden [2010] has another difference from Alg. 7.3. In Hardt and Rothblum [2010], Roth and Roughgarden [2010], the goal of using SVT is to determine whether the error of using an answer derived from past queries/answers is below a threshold. This check takes the form of "**if** $|\tilde{q}_i - q_i(D) + v_i| \geq T + \rho$ **then** output i," where $\tilde{q}_i$ gives the estimated answer of a query obtained using past queries/answers, and $q_i(D)$ gives the true answer. This is incorrect because the noise v_i should be outside the absolute value sign. In the usage in Hardt and Rothblum [2010], Roth and Roughgarden [2010], the left hand of the comparison is always ≥ 0; thus whenever the output includes at least one $\top$, one immediately knows that the threshold noise $\rho \geq -T$. This leakage of ρ is somewhat similar to Alg. 7.3's leakage caused by outputting noisy query answers that are found to be above the noisy threshold. This problem can be fixed by using "**if** $|\tilde{q}_i - q_i(D)| + v_i \geq$

$T + \rho$ **then** output i" instead. By viewing $r_i = |\tilde{q}_i - q_i(D)|$ as the query to be answered, this becomes a standard application of SVT.

7.3   OPTIMIZING SVT

Algorithm 7.1 can be viewed as allocating half of the privacy budget for perturbing the threshold and half for perturbing the query answers. This allocation is somewhat arbitrary, and other allocations are possible. Indeed, Algorithm 7.4 uses a ratio of 1 : 3 instead of 1 : 1. In this section, we study how to improve SVT by optimizing this allocation ratio and by introducing other techniques.

7.3.1   A GENERALIZED SVT ALGORITHM

Lyu et al. [2016] presented a generalized SVT algorithm in Algorithm 7.7, which uses ϵ_1 to perturb the threshold and ϵ_2 to perturb the query answers. Furthermore, to accommodate the situations where one wants the noisy counts for positive queries, we also use ϵ_3 to output query answers using the Laplace mechanism.

Algorithm 7.7 Standard SVT

Input: $D, Q, \Delta, \mathbf{T} = T_1, T_2, \cdots, c$ and ϵ_1, ϵ_2 and ϵ_3.
Output: A stream of answers $a_1, a_2, \cdots$

1: $\rho = \mathsf{Lap}\left(\frac{\Delta}{\epsilon_1}\right)$, count = 0
2: **for** Each query $q_i \in Q$ **do**
3:     $v_i = \mathsf{Lap}\left(\frac{2c\Delta}{\epsilon_2}\right)$
4:     **if** $q_i(D) + v_i \geq T_i + \rho$ **then**
5:         **if** $\epsilon_3 > 0$ **then**
6:             **Output** $a_i = q_i(D) + \mathsf{Lap}\left(\frac{c\Delta}{\epsilon_3}\right)$
7:         **else**
8:             **Output** $a_i = \top$
9:         **end if**
10:         count = count + 1, **Abort** if count $\geq c$.
11:     **else**
12:         **Output** $a_i = \bot$
13:     **end if**
14: **end for**

We now prove the privacy for Algorithm 7.7; the proof requires only minor changes from the proof of Theorem 7.2.

Theorem 7.6 *Algorithm 7.7 is* $(\epsilon_1 + \epsilon_2 + \epsilon_3)$-*DP.*

Proof. Algorithm 7.7 can be divided into two phases, the first phase outputs a vector to mark which query is above the threshold and the second phase uses the Laplace mechanism to output noisy counts. Since the second phase is ϵ_3-DP, it suffices to show that the first phase is $(\epsilon_1 + \epsilon_2)$-DP. For any output vector $\vec{a} \in \{\top, \bot\}^\ell$, we want to show

$$
\begin{aligned}
\Pr\left[\mathcal{A}(D) = \vec{a}\right] &= \int_{-\infty}^{\infty} \Pr[\rho = z] \ f_D(z) \ g_D(z) \, dz \\
&\leq \int_{-\infty}^{\infty} e^{\epsilon_1 + \epsilon_2} \Pr[\rho = z + \Delta] \ f_{D'}(z + \Delta) \ g_{D'}(z + \Delta) \, dz \\
&= e^{\epsilon_1 + \epsilon_2} \Pr\left[\mathcal{A}(D') = \vec{a}\right].
\end{aligned}
$$

This holds because, similarly to the proof of Theorem 7.2,

$$
\begin{aligned}
\Pr[\rho = z] &\leq e^{\epsilon_1} \Pr[\rho = z + \Delta], \\
f_D(z) &= \prod_{i \in I_\bot} \Pr[q_i(D) + v_i < T_i + z] \leq f_{D'}(z + \Delta), \\
g_D(z) &= \prod_{i \in I_\top} \Pr[q_i(D) + v_i \geq T_i + z] \leq e^{\epsilon_2} g_{D'}(z + \Delta).
\end{aligned}
$$

$\square$

7.3.2   OPTIMIZING PRIVACY BUDGET ALLOCATION

In Algorithm 7.7, one needs to decide how to divide up a total privacy budget ϵ into $\epsilon_1, \epsilon_2, \epsilon_3$. We note that $\epsilon_1 + \epsilon_2$ is used for outputting the indicator vector, and ϵ_3 is used for outputting the noisy counts for queries found to be above the threshold; thus the ratio of $(\epsilon_1 + \epsilon_2) : \epsilon_3$ is determined by the domain needs and should be an input to the algorithm.

On the other hand, the ratio of $\epsilon_1 : \epsilon_2$ affects the accuracy of SVT. Most variants use $1 : 1$, without a clear justification. To choose a ratio that can be justified, we observe that this ratio affects the accuracy of the following comparison:

$$
q_i(D) + \mathsf{Lap}\left(\frac{2c\Delta}{\epsilon_2}\right) \geq T + \mathsf{Lap}\left(\frac{\Delta}{\epsilon_1}\right).
$$

To make this comparison as accurate as possible, we want to minimize the variance of $\mathsf{Lap}\left(\frac{\Delta}{\epsilon_1}\right) - \mathsf{Lap}\left(\frac{2c\Delta}{\epsilon_2}\right)$, which is

$$
2\left(\frac{\Delta}{\epsilon_1}\right)^2 + 2\left(\frac{2c\Delta}{\epsilon_2}\right)^2,
$$

when $\epsilon_1 + \epsilon_2$ is fixed. This is minimized when

$$
\epsilon_1 : \epsilon_2 = 1 : (2c)^{2/3}. \tag{7.14}
$$

We will evaluate the improvement resulted from this optimization in Section 7.4.1.

7.3.3   SVT FOR MONOTONIC QUERIES

In some usages of SVT, the queries are monotonic. That is, when changing from D to D', all queries whose answers are different change in the same direction, i.e., there do not exist q_i, q_j such that $(q_i(D) > q_i(D')) \wedge (q_j(D) < q_j(D'))$. That is, we have either $\forall_i\, q_i(D) \geq q_i(D')$, or $\forall_i\, q_i(D') \geq q_i(D)$. This is the case when using SVT for frequent itemset mining in Lee and Clifton [2014] with neighboring datasets defined as adding or removing one tuple. For monotonic queries, adding $\mathsf{Lap}\left(\frac{c\Delta}{\epsilon_2}\right)$ instead of $\mathsf{Lap}\left(\frac{2c\Delta}{\epsilon_2}\right)$ suffices for privacy.

Theorem 7.7   *Algorithm 7.7 with $v_i = \mathsf{Lap}\left(\frac{c\Delta}{\epsilon_2}\right)$ in line 3 satisfies $(\epsilon_1 + \epsilon_2 + \epsilon_3)$-DP when all queries are monotonic.*

Proof. Because the second phase of Alg. 7.7 is still ϵ_3-DP, we just need to show that for any output vector $\vec{a}$,

$$\Pr\left[\mathcal{A}(D) = \vec{a}\right] = \int_{-\infty}^{\infty} \Pr\left[\rho = z\right]\ f_D(z)\ g_D(z)\, dz$$
$$\leq e^{\epsilon_1 + \epsilon_2} \Pr\left[\mathcal{A}(D') = \vec{a}\right],$$
$$\text{where}\ \ f_D(z) = \prod_{i \in I_\perp} \Pr\left[q_i(D) + v_i < T_i + z\right],$$
$$\text{and}\ \ g_D(z) = \prod_{i \in I_\top} \Pr\left[q_i(D) + v_i \geq T_i + z\right].$$

It suffices to show that either $\Pr\left[\rho = z\right] f_D(z)g_D(z) \leq e^{\epsilon_1 + \epsilon_2} \Pr\left[\rho = z\right] f_{D'}(z)g_{D'}(z)$, or $\Pr\left[\rho = z\right] f_D(z)g_D(z) \leq e^{\epsilon_1 + \epsilon_2} \Pr\left[\rho = z + \Delta\right] f_{D'}(z + \Delta)g_{D'}(z + \Delta)$. First consider the case that $q_i(D) \geq q_i(D')$ for any query q_i. In this case, we have

$$\Pr\left[q_i(D) + v_i < T_i + z\right] \leq \Pr\left[q_i(D') + v_i < T_i + z\right],$$

and thus $f_D(z) \leq f_{D'}(z)$. Note that $q_i(D) - q_i(D') \leq \Delta$. Therefore, $g_D(z) \leq e^{\epsilon_2} g_{D'}(z)$, without increasing the noisy threshold by Δ, because $\Pr\left[q_i(D) + v_i \geq T_i + z\right] \leq \Pr\left[q_i(D') + v_i \geq T_i + z - \Delta\right] \leq e^{\frac{\epsilon_2}{c}} \Pr\left[q_i(D') + v_i \geq T_i + z\right]$ since $v_i = \mathsf{Lap}\left(\frac{c\Delta}{\epsilon_2}\right)$. Then consider the case in which $q_i(D) \leq q_i(D')$ for any query q_i. We have the usual

$$f_D(z) \leq f_{D'}(z + \Delta),$$
$$\text{and}\ \Pr\left[\rho = z\right] \leq e^{\epsilon_1} \Pr\left[\rho = z + \Delta\right],$$

as in previous proofs. With the constraint $q_i(D) \leq q_i(D')$, using $v_i = \mathsf{Lap}\left(\frac{c\Delta}{\epsilon_2}\right)$ suffices to ensure that $\Pr\left[q_i(D) + v_i \geq T_i + z\right] \leq e^{\frac{\epsilon_2}{c}} \Pr\left[q_i(D') + v_i \geq T_i + \Delta + z\right]$. Thus $g_D(z) \leq e^{\epsilon_2} g_{D'}(z + \Delta)$ holds.   □

For monotonic queries, the optimization of privacy budget allocation (7.14) becomes $\epsilon_1 : \epsilon_2 = 1 : c^{2/3}$.

7.4   SVT VS. EM

We now discuss the application of SVT in the non-interactive setting, where all the queries are known ahead of time. We note that most recent usages of SVT, e.g., Chen et al. [2015], Lee and Clifton [2014], Shokri and Shmatikov [2015], Stoddard et al. [2014], Zhang et al. [2014a], are in the non-interactive setting. Furthermore, these applications of SVT aim at selecting up to c queries with the highest answers. In Lee and Clifton [2014], SVT is applied to find the c most frequent itemsets, where the queries are the supports for the itemsets. In Chen et al. [2015], the goal of using SVT is to determine the structure of a Bayesian network that preserves as much information of the dataset as possible. To this end, they select attribute groups that are highly correlated and create edges for such groups in the network. While the algorithm in Chen et al. [2015] takes the form of selecting attribute groups with a score above a certain threshold, the real goal is to select the groups with the highest scores. In Shokri and Shmatikov [2015], SVT is used to select parameters to be shared when trying to learn neural-network models in a private fashion. Once selected, noises are added to these parameters before they are shared. The selection step aims at selecting the parameters with the highest scores.

EM or SVT.   In a non-interactive setting, one can also use the Exponential Mechanism (EM) [McSherry and Talwar, 2007] to achieve the same objective of selecting the top c queries. More specifically, one runs EM c times, each round with privacy budget $\frac{\epsilon}{c}$. The quality for each query is its answer; thus each query is selected with probability proportion to $\exp\left(\frac{\epsilon}{2c\Delta}\right)$ in the general case and to $\exp\left(\frac{\epsilon}{c\Delta}\right)$ in the monotonic case. After one query is selected, it is removed from the pool of candidate queries for the remaining rounds.

An intriguing question is whether SVT or EM offers higher accuracy. Theorem 3.24 in Dwork and Roth [2013] regarding the utility of SVT with $c = \Delta = 1$ states: For any sequence of k queries $f_1, \ldots, f_k$ such that $|\{i < k : f_i(D) \geq T - \alpha\}| = 0$ (i.e., the only query close to being above threshold is possibly the last one), SVT is (α, β) accurate (meaning that with probability at least $1 - \beta$, all queries with answers below $T - \alpha$ result in $\perp$ and all queries with answers above $T - \alpha$ result in $\top$) for: $\alpha_{\text{SVT}} = 8(\log k + \log(2/\beta))/\epsilon$.

In the case where the last query is at least $T + \alpha$, being (α, β)-correct ensures that with probability at least $1 - \beta$, the correct selection is made. For the same setting, we say that *EM is (α, β)-correct* if given $k - 1$ queries with answer $\leq T - \alpha$ and one query with answer $\geq T + \alpha$, the correct selection is made with probability at least $1 - \beta$. The probability of selecting the query with answer $\geq T + \alpha$ is at least $\frac{e^{\epsilon(T+\alpha)/2}}{(k-1)e^{\epsilon(T-\alpha)/2} + e^{\epsilon(T+\alpha)/2}}$ by the definition of EM. To ensure this probability is at least $1 - \beta$,

$$\alpha_{\text{EM}} = (\log(k - 1) + \log((1 - \beta)/\beta))/\epsilon,$$

which is less than $1/8$ of the α_{SVT}, which suggests that EM is more accurate than SVT.

The above analysis relies on assuming that the first $k-1$ queries are no more than $T-\alpha$. When that is not assumed, it is difficult to analyze the utility of either SVT or EM. Therefore, we will use experimental methods to compare SVT with EM.

SVT with Retraversal. We want to find the most optimized version of SVT to compare with EM, and note that another interesting parameter that one can tune when applying SVT is that of the threshold T. When T is high, the algorithm may select fewer than c queries after traversing all queries. Since roughly each selected query consumes $\frac{1}{c}$'th of the privacy budget, outputting fewer than c queries kind of "wasted" the remaining privacy budget. When T is low, however, the algorithm may have selected c queries before encountering later queries. No matter how large some of these later query answers are, they cannot be selected.

We observe that in the non-interactive setting, there is a way to deal with this challenge. One can use a higher threshold T, and when the algorithm runs out of queries before finding c above-threshold queries, one can retraverse the list of queries that have not been selected so far, until c queries are selected. However, it is unclear how to select the optimal threshold.

7.4.1   EVALUATION

See Lyu et al. [2016] for experimental comparisons of different variants of SVT and with TM. The main findings are as follows. For the non-interactive setting, EM out-performs all SVT variants. For the interactive setting, where EM and SVT with retraversal cannot be used, the standard SVT algorithm performs better than previous SVT algorithms.

7.5   BIBLIOGRAPHICAL NOTES

SVT was introduced by Dwork et al. [2009], and improved by Roth and Roughgarden [2010] and by Hardt and Rothblum [2010]. These usages are in an interactive setting. An early description of SVT as a stand-alone technique appeared in Roth's 2011 lecture notes [Roth, 2011], which is Algorithm 7.3 in this chapter, and is in fact ∞-DP. The algorithms in Hardt and Rothblum [2010], Roth and Roughgarden [2010] also have another difference, as discussed in Section 7.2.4. Another version of SVT appeared in the 2014 book [Dwork and Roth, 2013], which is Algorithm 7.2. This version is used in some papers, e.g., Shokri and Shmatikov [2015]. It is possible to add less noise and obtain higher accuracy for the same privacy parameter.

Lee and Clifton [2014] used a variant of SVT (see Algorithm 7.4) to find itemsets whose support is above the threshold. Stoddard et al. [2014] proposed another variant (see Algorithm 7.5) for private feature selection for classification to pick out the set of features with scores greater than the perturbed threshold. Chen et al. [2015] employed yet another variant of SVT (see Algorithm 7.6) to return attribute pairs with mutual information greater than the corresponding noisy threshold. These usages are not private.

Some of these errors were pointed in Chen and Machanavajjhala [2015], in which a generalized private threshold testing algorithm (GPTT) that attempts to model the SVT variants in

Chen et al. [2015], Lee and Clifton [2014], Stoddard et al. [2014] was introduced. The authors showed that GPTT did not satisfy ϵ'-DP for any finite ϵ'. But there is an error in the proof, as shown in Section 7.2.3. Zhang et al. [2014b] presented two proofs that the variant of SVT violates DP without discussing the cause of the errors.

This chapter is mostly based on Lyu et al. [2016], which introduced the general version of improved SVT (Algorithm 7.1 and Algorithm 7.7), the techniques of optimizing budget allocation, the technique of using re-traversal to improve SVT, and the comparison of SVT and EM.

Bibliography

Gergely Acs, Claude Castelluccia, and Rui Chen. Differentially private histogram publishing through lossy compression. In *ICDM*, pages 1–10, 2012. DOI: 10.1109/icdm.2012.80. 59, 60

Charu C. Aggarwal. On k-anonymity and the curse of dimensionality. In *VLDB*, pages 901–909, 2005. 54

Sanjeev Arora, Elad Hazan, and Satyen Kale. The multiplicative weights update method: A meta algorithm and applications. *Theory of Computing*, 8, pages 121–164, 2012. 5

Boaz Barak, Kamalika Chaudhuri, Cynthia Dwork, Satyen Kale, Frank McSherry, and Kunal Talwar. Privacy, accuracy, and consistency too: A holistic solution to contingency table release. In *PODS*, pages 273–282, 2007. DOI: 10.1145/1265530.1265569. 81, 86, 87, 91

Michael Barbaro and Jr. Tom Zeller. A face is exposed for aol searcher no. 4417749. New York Times, Aug 2006. 3, 42

Raghav Bhaskar, Srivatsan Laxman, Adam Smith, and Abhradeep Thakurta. Discovering frequent patterns in sensitive data. In *KDD*, pages 503–512, 2010. DOI: 10.1145/1835804.1835869. 5

E. J. Bloustein. *Individual & Group Privacy*. Transaction Publishers, 2002. ISBN 9781412826204. 42

Avrim Blum, Cynthia Dwork, Frank McSherry, and Kobbi Nissim. Practical privacy: The SuLQ framework. In *PODS*, pages 128–138, 2005. DOI: 10.1145/1065167.1065184. 30, 70

Alexandra Boldyreva, Nathan Chenette, Younho Lee, and Adam O'Neill. Order-preserving symmetric encryption. In *Proc. of the 28th Annual International Conference on Advances in Cryptology: The Theory and Applications of Cryptographic Techniques*, EUROCRYPT'09, pages 224–241, Berlin, Heidelberg, 2009. Springer-Verlag. ISBN 978-3-642-01000-2. http://dx.doi.org/10.1007/978-3-642-01001-9_13 DOI: 10.1007/978-3-642-01001-9_13. 35

Kamalika Chaudhuri and Claire Monteleoni. Privacy-preserving logistic regression. In *NIPS*, pages 289–296, 2008. 64, 65, 66

Kamalika Chaudhuri, Claire Monteleoni, and Anand D. Sarwate. Differentially private empirical risk minimization. *The Journal of Machine Learning Research*, 12, pages 1069–1109, 2011. 65, 66

Rui Chen, Qian Xiao, Yu Zhang, and Jianliang Xu. Differentially private high-dimensional data publication via sampling-based inference. In *KDD*, pages 129–138, 2015. DOI: 10.1145/2783258.2783379. 93, 94, 95, 97, 102, 103, 104, 106, 110, 111, 112

Yan Chen and Ashwin Machanavajjhala. On the privacy properties of variants on the sparse vector technique. *CoRR*, abs/1508.07306, 2015. http://arxiv.org/abs/1508.07306 94, 104, 106, 111

Mahdi Cheraghchi, Adam Klivans, Pravesh Kothari, and Homin K. Lee. Submodular functions are noise stable. In *SODA*, pages 1586–1592, 2012. DOI: 10.1137/1.9781611973099.126. 83

G. Cormode, M. Procopiuc, E. Shen, D. Srivastava, and T. Yu. Differentially private spatial decompositions. In *ICDE*, pages 258–269, 2012. DOI: 10.1109/icde.2012.16. 59

Graham Cormode, Divesh Srivastava, Ninghui Li, and Tiancheng Li. Minimizing minimality and maximizing utility: Analyzing method-based attacks on anonymized data. *Proc. VLDB Endow.*, 3(1–2), pages 1045–1056, September 2010. DOI: 10.14778/1920841.1920972. 33

T. Dalenius. Towards a methodology for statistical disclosure control. *Statistik Tidskrift*, 15(429–444), pages 2–1, 1977. 34

Bolin Ding, Marianne Winslett, Jiawei Han, and Zhenhui Li. Differentially private data cubes: Optimizing noise sources and consistency. In *SIGMOD Conference*, pages 217–228, 2011. DOI: 10.1145/1989323.1989347. 82

Irit Dinur and Kobbi Nissim. Revealing information while preserving privacy. In *PODS*, pages 202–210, 2003. DOI: 10.1145/773153.773173. 30, 31, 93

Charles Duhigg. How companies learn your secrets. *New York Times Magazine*, February 2012. http://www.nytimes.com/2012/02/19/magazine/shopping-habits.html 44

C. Dwork and S. Yekhanin. New efficient attacks on statistical disclosure control mechanisms. *Advances in Cryptology—CRYPTO 2008*, pages 469–480, 2008. DOI: 10.1007/978-3-540-85174-5_26. 30, 93

C. Dwork, M. Naor, O. Reingold, G. N. Rothblum, and S. Vadhan. On the complexity of differentially private data release: Efficient algorithms and hardness results. *STOC*, pages 381–390, 2009. DOI: 10.1145/1536414.1536467. 30, 93, 111

C. Dwork, G. Rothblum, and S. Vadhan. Boosting and differential privacy. *Foundations of Computer Science (FOCS), 2010 51st Annual IEEE Symposium on*, pages 51–60, 2010. DOI: 10.1109/focs.2010.12. 83, 106

Cynthia Dwork. Differential privacy. In *ICALP*, pages 1–12, 2006. DOI: 10.1007/11787006_1. 7, 31, 35, 44

Cynthia Dwork. Differential privacy: A survey of results. In *TAMC*, pages 1–19, 2008. DOI: 10.1007/978-3-540-79228-4_1. 1

Cynthia Dwork. A firm foundation for private data analysis. *Commun. ACM*, 54(1), pages 86–95, 2011. DOI: 10.1145/1866739.1866758. 69

Cynthia Dwork and Moni Naor. On the difficulties of disclosure prevention in statistical databases or the case for differential privacy. *Journal of Privacy and Confidentiality*, 2, 2008. 35, 44

Cynthia Dwork and Kobbi Nissim. Privacy-preserving datamining on vertically partitioned databases. In *CRYPTO*, pages 528–544, 2004. DOI: 10.1007/978-3-540-28628-8_32. 31

Cynthia Dwork and Aaron Roth. The algorithmic foundations of differential privacy. *Theoretical Computer Science*, 9(3–4), pages 211–407, 2013. DOI: 10.1561/0400000042. 1, 34, 94, 95, 96, 100, 110, 111

Cynthia Dwork and Adam Smith. Differential privacy for statistics: What we know and what we want to learn. *Journal of Privacy and Confidentiality*, 1(2), page 2, 2010. 1, 43

Cynthia Dwork, Frank McSherry, Kobbi Nissim, and Adam Smith. Calibrating noise to sensitivity in private data analysis. In *TCC*, pages 265–284, 2006. DOI: 10.1007/11681878_14. 7, 12, 30, 31, 38, 39, 68, 81, 93, 106

Cynthia Dwork, Frank McSherry, and Kunal Talwar. The price of privacy and the limits of LP decoding. In *STOC*, pages 85–94, 2007. DOI: 10.1145/1250790.1250804. 30, 93

Úlfar Erlingsson, Vasyl Pihur, and Aleksandra Korolova. Rappor: Randomized aggregatable privacy-preserving ordinal response. In *Proc. of the 2014 ACM SIGSAC Conference on Computer and Communications Security*, CCS'14, pages 1054–1067, 2014. DOI: 10.1145/2660267.2660348. 40

Arik Friedman and Assaf Schuster. Data mining with differential privacy. In *KDD*, pages 493–502, 2010. DOI: 10.1145/1835804.1835868. 70

Srivatsava Ranjit Ganta, Shiva Prasad Kasiviswanathan, and Adam Smith. Composition attacks and auxiliary information in data privacy. In *KDD*, pages 265–273, 2008. DOI: 10.1145/1401890.1401926. 36, 44

Shafi Goldwasser and Silvio Micali. Probabilistic encryption. *Journal of Computer and System Sciences*, 28(2), pages 270–299, 1984. DOI: 10.1016/0022-0000(84)90070-9. 35

Dan Gordon. La jolla covering repository, November 2012. http://www.ccrwest.org/cover.html 91

Anupam Gupta, Moritz Hardt, Aaron Roth, and Jonathan Ullman. Privately releasing conjunctions and the statistical query barrier. In *STOC*, pages 803–812, 2011. DOI: 10.1145/1993636.1993742. 82, 83

Anupam Gupta, Aaron Roth, and Jonathan Ullman. Iterative constructions and private data release. In *TCC*, pages 339–356, 2012a. DOI: 10.1007/978-3-642-28914-9_19. 83

Anupam Gupta, Aaron Roth, and Jonathan Ullman. Iterative constructions and private data release. In *TCC*, pages 339–356, 2012b. DOI: 10.1007/978-3-642-28914-9_19. 93, 94, 100

Moritz Hardt and Guy N. Rothblum. A multiplicative weights mechanism for privacy-preserving data analysis. In *FOCS*, pages 61–70, 2010. Full version at http://www.mrtz.org/papers/HR10mult.pdf. DOI: 10.1109/focs.2010.85. 30, 82, 93, 94, 100, 106, 111

Moritz Hardt and Kunal Talwar. On the geometry of differential privacy. In *Proc. of the 42nd ACM symposium on Theory of computing*, STOC'10, pages 705–714, New York, NY, 2010. ACM. ISBN 978-1-4503-0050-6. DOI: 10.1145/1806689.1806786. 30

Moritz Hardt, Katrina Ligett, and Frank McSherry. A simple and practical algorithm for differentially private data release. In *NIPS*, pages 2348–2356, 2012. 5, 82, 83, 91

Michael Hay, Vibhor Rastogi, Gerome Miklau, and Dan Suciu. Boosting the accuracy of differentially private histograms through consistency. *PVLDB*, 3(1), pages 1021–1032, 2010. DOI: 10.14778/1920841.1920970. 60, 88

Michael Hay, Ashwin Machanavajjhala, Gerome Miklau, Yan Chen, and Dan Zhang. Principled evaluation of differentially private algorithms using dpbench. In *SIGMOD*, 2016. DOI: 10.1145/2882903.2882931. 60

Nils Homer, Szabolcs Szelinger, Margot Redman, David Duggan, Waibhav Tembe, Jill Muehling, John V. Pearson, Dietrich A. Stephan, Stanley F. Nelson, and David W. Craig. Resolving individuals contributing trace amounts of DNA to highly complex mixtures using high-density SNP genotyping microarrays. *PLoS Genet*, 4(8), page e1000167+, 08 2008. DOI: 10.1371/journal.pgen.1000167. 3

Justin Hsu, Marco Gaboardi, Andreas Haeberlen, Sanjeev Khanna, Arjun Narayan, Benjamin C. Pierce, and Aaron Roth. Differential privacy: An economic method for choosing epsilon. In *IEEE 27th Computer Security Foundations Symposium, CSF 2014, Vienna, Austria, 19–22 July, 2014*, pages 398–410, 2014. DOI: 10.1109/csf.2014.35. 43

Zhanglong Ji, Zachary C. Lipton, and Charles Elkan. Differential privacy and machine learning: A survey and review. *CoRR*, abs/1412.7584, 2014. 1

Shiva Prasad Kasiviswanathan and Adam Smith. A note on differential privacy: Defining resistance to arbitrary side information. *CoRR*, abs/0803.3946, 2008. 36, 44

Shiva Prasad Kasiviswanathan and Adam Smith. On the "semantics" of differential privacy: A Bayesian formulation. *Journal of Privacy and Confidentiality*, 6(1), pages 1–16, 2014. 36, 44

Daniel Kifer and Ashwin Machanavajjhala. No free lunch in data privacy. In *SIGMOD*, pages 193–204, 2011. DOI: 10.1145/1989323.1989345. 7, 35, 38, 44

Jaewoo Lee and Christopher W. Clifton. Top-k frequent itemsets via differentially private fp-trees. In *KDD'14*, pages 931–940, 2014. DOI: 10.1145/2623330.2623723. 93, 94, 95, 96, 102, 103, 104, 106, 109, 110, 111, 112

Jing Lei. Differentially private m-estimators. In *NIPS*, pages 361–369, 2011. 74, 75, 81

Chao Li and Gerome Miklau. An adaptive mechanism for accurate query answering under differential privacy. *Proc. VLDB Endow.*, 5(6), pages 514–525, February 2012. DOI: 10.14778/2168651.2168653. 53

Chao Li, Michael Hay, Vibhor Rastogi, Gerome Miklau, and Andrew McGregor. Optimizing linear counting queries under differential privacy. In *Proc. of the twenty-ninth ACM SIGMOD-SIGACT-SIGART Symposium on Principles of Database Systems*, PODS'10, pages 123–134, New York, NY, 2010. ACM. ISBN 978-1-4503-0033-9. DOI: 10.1145/1807085.1807104. 53

Chao Li, Michael Hay, Gerome Miklau, and Yue Wang. A data-and workload-aware algorithm for range queries under differential privacy. *PVLDB*, 7(5), 2014a. DOI: 10.14778/2732269.2732271. 58, 60

Muyuan Li, Haojin Zhu, Zhaoyu Gao, Si Chen, Le Yu, Shangqian Hu, and Kui Ren. All your location are belong to us: Breaking mobile social networks for automated user location tracking. In *Proc. of the 15th ACM International Symposium on Mobile Ad Hoc Networking and Computing*, MobiHoc'14, pages 43–52, 2014b. DOI: 10.1145/2632951.2632953. 3, 4

Ninghui Li, Tiancheng Li, and Suresh Venkatasubramanian. t-Closeness: Privacy beyond k-anonymity and ℓ-diversity. In *ICDE*, pages 106–115, 2007. DOI: 10.1109/icde.2007.367856. 33

Ninghui Li, Wahbeh Qardaji, and Dong Su. On sampling, anonymization, and differential privacy or, k-anonymization meets differential privacy. In *ASIACCS*, 2012a. The initial official proceedings includes only a 2-page summary for every paper. Complete paper was later added to ACM DL, and is available at http://delivery.acm.org/10.1145/2420000/2414474/p32-li.pdf. DOI: 10.1145/2414456.2414474. 33, 44

Ninghui Li, Wahbeh H. Qardaji, Dong Su, and Jianneng Cao. Privbasis: Frequent itemset mining with differential privacy. *PVLDB*, 5(11), pages 1340–1351, 2012b. DOI: 10.14778/2350229.2350251. 6

Ninghui Li, Wahbeh H. Qardaji, Dong Su, Yi Wu, and Weining Yang. Membership privacy: A unifying framework for privacy definitions. In *2013 ACM SIGSAC Conference on Computer and Communications Security, CCS'13, Berlin, Germany, November 4–8, 2013*, pages 889–900, 2013. DOI: 10.1145/2508859.2516686. 35, 44

J. Lin. Divergence measures based on the shannon theory. *IEEE T. Infom. Theory*, 37, 1991. DOI: 10.1109/18.61115. 80

Stuart P. Lloyd. Least squares quantization in pcm. *IEEE Transactions on Information Theory*, 28(2), pages 129–136, 1982. DOI: 10.1109/tit.1982.1056489. 62

Min Lyu, Dong Su, and Ninghui Li. Understanding the sparse vector technique for differential privacy, 2016. arXiv:1603.01699. 107, 111, 112

Ashwin Machanavajjhala, Johannes Gehrke, Daniel Kifer, and Muthuramakrishnan Venkita-subramaniam. ℓ-diversity: Privacy beyond k-anonymity. In *ICDE*, page 24, 2006. DOI: 10.1109/icde.2006.1. 33

Frank McSherry. Privacy integrated queries (pinq) infrastructure. Available at `http://research.microsoft.com/en-us/downloads/73099525-fd8d-4966-9b93-574e6023147f/`. 23, 68

Frank McSherry. Privacy integrated queries: An extensible platform for privacy-preserving data analysis. In *SIGMOD*, pages 19–30, 2009. DOI: 10.1145/1559845.1559850. 31, 68

Frank McSherry and Ratul Mahajan. Differentially-private network trace analysis. *SIGCOMM Comput. Commun. Rev.*, 40(4), pages 123–134, August 2010. DOI: 10.1145/1851275.1851199. 40

Frank McSherry and Ilya Mironov. Differentially private recommender systems: Building privacy into the netflix prize contenders. In *KDD*, pages 627–636, 2009. DOI: 10.1145/1557019.1557090. 40

Frank McSherry and Kunal Talwar. Mechanism design via differential privacy. In *FOCS*, pages 94–103, 2007. DOI: 10.1109/focs.2007.66. 16, 20, 31, 94, 95, 110

Noman Mohammed, Rui Chen, Benjamin C. M. Fung, and Philip S. Yu. Differentially private data release for data mining. In *KDD*, pages 493–501, 2011. DOI: 10.1145/2020408.2020487. 75

Prashanth Mohan, Abhradeep Thakurta, Elaine Shi, Dawn Song, and David E. Culler. Gupt: Privacy preserving data analysis made easy. In *SIGMOD'12*, pages 349–360, 2012. DOI: 10.1145/2213836.2213876. 69

Arvind Narayanan and Vitaly Shmatikov. Robust de-anonymization of large sparse datasets. In *S&P*, pages 111–125, 2008. DOI: 10.1109/sp.2008.33. 3

Kobbi Nissim, Sofya Raskhodnikova, and Adam Smith. Smooth sensitivity and sampling in private data analysis. In *STOC*, pages 75–84, 2007. DOI: 10.1145/1250790.1250803. 62

OECD. Oecd privacy principles. http://oecdprivacy.org/ 38

J. M. Peña, J. A. Lozano, and P. Larrañaga. An empirical comparison of four initialization methods for the k-means algorithm. *Pattern Recogn. Lett.*, 20(10), pages 1027–1040, 1999. DOI: 10.1016/s0167-8655(99)00069-0. 69

Richard A. Posner. *Economic Analysis of Law*. Aspen, 1998. DOI: 10.2307/1227682. 34

Wahbeh Qardaji and Ninghui Li. Recursive partitioning and summarization: A practical framework for differential private data publishing. In *ASIACCS*, 2012. DOI: 10.1145/2414456.2414477. 60

Wahbeh Qardaji, Weining Yang, and Ninghui Li. Understanding hierarchical methods for differentially private histograms. *PVLDB*, 6(14), pages 1954–1965, 2013a. DOI: 10.14778/2556549.2556576. 48, 51, 52, 60

Wahbeh Qardaji, Weining Yang, and Ninghui Li. Differentially private grids for geospatial data. In *ICDE*, pages 757–768, 2013b. ISBN 978-1-4673-4909-3. DOI: 10.1109/icde.2013.6544872. 55, 56, 57, 60

Wahbeh Qardaji, Weining Yang, and Ninghui Li. Priview: Practical differentially private release of marginal contingency tables. In *Proc. of the 2014 ACM SIGMOD International Conference on Management of Data*, pages 1435–1446. ACM, 2014. DOI: 10.1145/2588555.2588575. 85, 87, 89, 90, 91

Wahbeh H. Qardaji, Weining Yang, and Ninghui Li. Differentially private grids for geospatial data. In *29th IEEE International Conference on Data Engineering (ICDE)*, pages 757–768, 2013c. DOI: 10.1109/icde.2013.6544872. 74

Vibhor Rastogi and Suman Nath. Differentially private aggregation of distributed time-series with transformation and encryption. In *SIGMOD*, pages 735–746, 2010. DOI: 10.1145/1807167.1807247. 58, 59

Aaron Roth. The sparse vector technique, 2011. http://www.cis.upenn.edu/~aaroth/courses/slides/Lecture11.pdf Lecture notes for "The Algorithmic Foundations of Data Privacy." 94, 95, 96, 100, 101, 111

Aaron Roth and Tim Roughgarden. Interactive privacy via the median mechanism. In *STOC*, pages 765–774, 2010. DOI: 10.1145/1806689.1806794. 30, 93, 106, 111

Benjamin I. P. Rubinstein, Peter L. Bartlett, Ling Huang, and Nina Taf. Protecting respondent's privacy in microdata release. *Journal of Privacy and Confidentiality*, 4(1), pages 65–100, 2012. 64

Pierangela Samarati. Protecting respondent's privacy in microdata release. *TKDE*, 13(6), pages 1010–1027, 2001. DOI: 10.1109/69.971193. 33

Reza Shokri and Vitaly Shmatikov. Privacy-preserving deep learning. In *CCS*, pages 1310–1321, 2015. DOI: 10.1109/allerton.2015.7447103. 93, 94, 95, 106, 110, 111

Daniel J. Solove. *Understanding Privacy*. Harvard University Press, 2010. 34

Ben Stoddard, Yan Chen, and Ashwin Machanavajjhala. Differentially private algorithms for empirical machine learning. *CoRR*, abs/1411.5428, 2014. 93, 94, 95, 97, 102, 103, 104, 106, 110, 111, 112

Dong Su, Jianneng Cao, and Ninghui Li. Privpfc: Differentially private data publication for classification, 2016a. arXiv:1504.05997. 75, 76

Dong Su, Jianneng Cao, Ninghui Li, Elisa Bertino, and Hongxia Jin. Differentially private k-means clustering. In *Proc. of the 6th ACM on Conference on Data and Application Security and Privacy, CODASPY*, pages 26–37, 2016b. DOI: 10.1145/2857705.2857708. 74, 76

Latanya Sweeney. *k*-anonymity: A model for protecting privacy. *Int. J. Uncertain. Fuzziness Knowl.-Based Syst.*, 10(5), pages 557–570, 2002. DOI: 10.1142/s0218488502001648. 2, 33, 42

Justin Thaler, Jonathan Ullman, and Salil P. Vadhan. Faster algorithms for privately releasing marginals. In *Automata, Languages, and Programming—39th International Colloquium, ICALP 2012, Warwick, UK, July 9-13, 2012, Proceedings, Part I*, pages 810–821, 2012. DOI: 10.1007/978-3-642-31594-7_68. 83, 84, 91

Stanley L. Warner. Randomized response: A survey technique for eliminating evasive answer bias. *Journal of the American Statistical Association*, 60(309), pages 63–69, 1965. DOI: 10.1080/01621459.1965.10480775. 30, 40

Samuel Warren and Louis Brandeis. The right to privacy. *Harvard Law Review*, 4, pages 193–220, 1890. DOI: 10.2307/1321160. 34

Alan F. Westin. *Privacy and Freedom*. Atheneum, 1967. 34

Charles Wheelan. *Naked Economics: Undressing the Dismal Science (Fully Revised and Updated)*. W. W. Norton & Company, 2010. 44

Raymond Chi-Wing Wong, Ada Wai-Chee Fu, Ke Wang, and Jian Pei. Minimality attack in privacy preserving data publishing. In *VLDB*, pages 543–554, 2007. 33

Xiaokui Xiao, Guozhang Wang, and Johannes Gehrke. Differential privacy via wavelet transforms. *IEEE Trans. Knowl. Data Eng.*, 23(8), pages 1200–1214, 2011. DOI: 10.1109/tkde.2010.247. 52

Y. Xiao, L. Xiong, and C. Yuan. Differential private data release through multidimensional partitioning. In *VLDB SDM Workshop*, 2010. DOI: 10.1007/978-3-642-15546-8_11. 59

Jia Xu, Zhenjie Zhang, Xiaokui Xiao, Yin Yang, and Ge Yu. Differentially private histogram publication. In *ICDE*, pages 32–43, 2012. DOI: 10.1109/icde.2012.48. 58

Ganzhao Yuan, Zhenjie Zhang, Marianne Winslett, Xiaokui Xiao, Yin Yang, and Zhifeng Hao. Low-rank mechanism: Optimizing batch queries under differential privacy. *PVLDB*, 5(11), pages 1352–1363, 2012. DOI: 10.14778/2350229.2350252. 53

Chen Zeng, Jeffrey F. Naughton, and Jin-Yi Cai. On differentially private frequent itemset mining. *Proc. VLDB Endow.*, 6(1), pages 25–36, November 2012. DOI: 10.14778/2428536.2428539. 5, 6

Jun Zhang, Zhenjie Zhang, Xiaokui Xiao, Yin Yang, and Marianne Winslett. Functional mechanism: Regression analysis under differential privacy. *PVLDB*, 5(11), pages 1364–1375, 2012. DOI: 10.14778/2350229.2350253. 66, 67

Jun Zhang, Xiaokui Xiao, Yin Yang, Zhenjie Zhang, and Marianne Winslett. Privgene: Differentially private model fitting using genetic algorithms. In *SIGMOD'13*, pages 665–676, 2013. DOI: 10.1145/2463676.2465330. 71, 72, 76

Jun Zhang, Graham Cormode, Cecilia M. Procopiuc, Divesh Srivastava, and Xiaokui Xiao. Privbayes: Private data release via bayesian networks. In *SIGMOD'14*, pages 1423–1434, 2014a. DOI: 10.1145/2588555.2588573. 110

Jun Zhang, Xiaokui Xiao, and Xing Xie. Privtree: A differentially private algorithm for hierarchical decompositions. In *SIGMOD'16*, 2014b. DOI: 10.1145/2882903.2882928. 94, 101, 103, 112

Authors' Biographies

NINGHUI LI

Ninghui Li is a professor of computer science at Purdue University. His research interests are in security and privacy. He received a Bachelor's degree from the University of Science and Technology of China in 1993 and a Ph.D. in computer science from New York University in 2000. Before joining the faculty of Purdue in 2003, he was a research associate at Stanford University's Computer Science Department for three years. Prof. Li is Vice Chair of ACM Special Interest Group on Security, Audit and Control (SIGSAC). He is serving, or has served, on the editorial boards of *ACM Transactions on Privacy and Security* (TOPS), *Journal of Computer Security* (JCS), *IEEE Transactions on Dependable and Secure Computing*, *VLDB Journal*, and *ACM Transactions on Internet Technology*. He has served on the Program Committees of many international conferences and workshops in computer security, databases, and data mining, including serving as Program Chair for 2014 and 2015 ACM Conference on Computer and Communications Security (CCS), ACM's flagship conference in the field of security and privacy.

MIN LYU

Min Lyu has been a lecturer in the School of Computer Science and Technology at the University of Science and Technology of China since 2007. She received a Bachelor's degree and a Master's degree in applied mathematics from Anhui University in 1999 and 2002, respectively, and a Ph.D. in applied mathematics from the University of Science and Technology of China in 2005. Before joining the faculty of the University of Science and Technology of China in 2007, she was a post-doctor in School of Computer Science and Technology at the University of Science and Technology of China for two years. She was a visiting scholar at Purdue University in 2015, hosted by Professor Ninghui Li on the topic of differential privacy. Her research interests are in security and privacy, social networks, and combinatorial mathematics.

DONG SU

Dong Su is a Ph.D. student in the Computer Science Department at Purdue University. He received a Bachelor's degree in software engineering from Tianjin University in 2005 and a Master's degree in computer science from the University of Chinese Academy of Sciences in 2010. He entered Purdue University in the Fall of 2010, and is working under the supervision of Dr. Ninghui

Li on the topic of differentially private data publishing for data analysis. His research interests are in data privacy, information security, machine learning, and database management systems.

WEINING YANG

Weining Yang is a Ph.D. student in the Department of Computer Science at Purdue University. He attended Tsinghua University and graduated with a Bachelor's degree in computer science in 2011. He entered Purdue University in the Fall of 2011, and worked under the supervision of Dr. Ninghui Li on the topic of differentially private data publishing and password-based authentication. His research interests are in security and privacy, in particular private data publishing and user authentication.

Printed in the United States
by Baker & Taylor Publisher Services